YOUR DREAM CREATES YOUR FUTURE

Unveiling The Creative Power Of Positive And Possibility Mentality

SUNDAY A. EZEKIEL

Copyright © 2014 by: Sunday A. Ezekiel

Repackaged, edited and reprinted in 2017

Published in Nigeria by: DW-Impact Ltd, Lagos – Nigeria

All rights reserved. No portion of this publication may be reproduced, stored in retrieval system, or transmitted in any form by any means – electronic, mechanical, photocopying, recording, or any other – without the prior written permission of the publisher, except for brief quotations in printed reviews, magazines, articles etc.

For further enquiries, distribution or permission, contact:

Dreamers World Christian Centre

Phone: +234-8035122385, +234-7082982341

Email: info@dreamersworldng.org

Website: www.dreamersworldng.org

Facebook Pages: Dreamers World Christian Centre

Dream Big & Succeed Dreamers World International

All Scripture quotations are from the King James Version of the Bible, except otherwise stated.

CONTENTS

DEDICATION 7

INTRODUCTION 9

PART ONE 16

Chapter 1: IT IS THE DREAMERS' WORLD 18

Chapter 2: THE NATURE OF DREAMS 33

Chapter 3: DREAMS ARE MENTAL PROJECTIONS 67

PART TWO 90

Chapter 4: DISCOVER YOUR PURPOSE 93

Chapter 5: DISCOVER AND RELEASE YOUR POTENTIAL 109

Chapter 6: DOCUMENT YOUR DREAM...............126

Chapter 7: DEVELOP A PLAN 142

Chapter 8: DECISIONS: THE KEY FACTORS 162

Chapter 9: DARE YOUR DREAM 195

Chapter 10: PATIENCE OF PURPOSE.................232

PART THREE 255

Chapter 11: FEAR 257

Chapter 12: PROCRASTINATION.......................266

Chapter 13: PRIDE..285

Chapter 14: SELF-CENTEREDNESS 296

Chapter 15: IMPATIENCE 307

THE FINAL WORD 317

GET CONNECTED...324

Other Books By The Same Author 327

About The Author 328

DEDICATION

This book is dedicated to:

- God, the Father and Source of all great dreams;

- Jesus Christ, my Lord and King

- The Holy Spirit, the Chief Executor of divine dreams on earth;

- Dr. David Oyedepo, my father in the faith, mentor in ministry and a great dreamer with a heart for God;

- All great dreamers whose dreams have given shape to the shapeless world;

- And to all men whose dreams will be unleashed as solutions to the world's problems as they read this book.

INTRODUCTION

If you can imagine it, you can achieve it. If you can dream it, you can become it. - William Arthur Ward

Dreams are seeds of great accomplishments and fulfillment in life. Success in every endeavour of man is traceable to the dream of man. To put it in another way; no man can fulfill a divine mandate without engaging the power of dream. In other words, the reason for failure in the race of life is a direct product of lack of dream. One person with a dream can accomplish more than one hundred others without one.

Zig Ziglar, a proven author and international speaker on this subject said; *"If you can dream it, then you can achieve it."*

That simply means that, you cannot achieve what you do not dream. I like to put it this way; *"Your achievement in life is a direct product of your dream; no more, no less"*.

All through the years of my research and study of the subject of greatness and success achievement, I have come to the conclusion that no man on this planet earth can talk about great accomplishment in the absence of a great dream.

I believe that the twenty-first century's great accomplishment will outweigh those of earlier centuries; but the truth is that twenty-first century men must learn how to dream greater dreams and follow after their dreams.

The great man, Henry David Thoreau said; *"If one advances confidently in the direction of his dreams, and endeavors to live the life which he has imagined, he will meet with success unexpected in common hours. He will put some things behind, will pass an invisible boundary; new, universal, and more liberal laws will begin to establish themselves around and within him; or old laws will be expanded and interpreted in his favor in a more liberal sense, and he will live with a license of a higher order of beings"*

That is why the revelation and principles in this book are very essential to the fulfillment of people from different walks of life, because it is the reality of a dream of many years ago. The fact that you are reading this book is evident that whatever you can dream, you can achieve.

However, I believe that, in this book, you will not only know what dream means, but you will also know the practical steps you must take to fulfill your own. Also, you will learn about great dreamers whose dreams have become realities so that you can follow their footsteps to turn your own dream into reality.

Moreover, you will learn how powerful your own dream can be and that you can accomplish even more than what your present dream is. And finally, I will be showing you the constraints, limiting factors and pot-holes on the road to turning your dream into reality so that you can guard against them.

Please understand that dreamers are leaders. The man who can dream is the man who can lead. Show me a great dreamer today and I will show you a great leader tomorrow. From obscurity, Joseph emerged the greatest leader in Egypt. But remember that many years before then, it was said concerning him that he had a dream (Genesis 37:5, 6, 9)

In the same way, every empire on earth today is a reality of yesterday's dream in the heart of someone who has emerged as a great leader today. Your dream of today will create a future for you as long as you follow it and keep it from being aborted.

What is that dream in your heart right now? Do you believe it can become a reality tomorrow? Do you know that your dream can impact your generation if you follow it with all your God given abilities? Do you know that falling down or failing at one time or the other is part of the process you need to pass through in fulfilling your dream?

Please follow me carefully through the pages of this book as these questions are answered with all simplicity.

I have a charge to the body of Christ that the wealth in the hands of sinners in the world are reserved for the believers in this end time; we are right in the center of the prophetic season of supernatural wealth transfer, but we can only take delivery of this enormous wealth by covenant dreams provoked by divine inspiration. (Proverbs 13:22 & Eph. 3:20)

This book will show you the practicality of dream power. And as you take time to digest the truth therein, the world will soon celebrate the reality of your own dream.

Friend, sit tight, it is time to take off on this flight of great accomplishment as you begin to dream big and pursue your big dream. You are the architect of your own destiny by your dream.

You can do anything you want to do; you can be anything you want to be. You can go anywhere from where you are- if you are willing to dream big and work hard.

ROBERT SCHULLER

PART ONE

UNDERSTANDING THE POWER OF DREAM

Dreams are powerful in creating a future for man. That is why everyone who desires a great future needs to have a very good understanding of the subject of dream.

It is a well known truth that every empire in the world today is built by a dream in the heart of man. Also, there are still great empires that will be built in this world as products of the great dreams in the hearts of certain men who do not look like great men now.

However, in this first part of the book, I will introduce to you the great wonders that the world has experienced by virtue of man's dreams.

Also, you will have an understanding of the nature of dreams and how powerful your mental projections can be in changing your circumstances into what you desire.

If you really desire to move from where you are now to a better place, your ability to dream a different type of dream is the key. That is why **YOU MUST HAVE A DREAM.**

Chapter 1: IT IS THE DREAMERS' WORLD

If you can dream it, you can do it. Always remember that this whole thing was started with a dream and a mouse

WALT DISNEY

Most men die from the neck up by the age of 25, because they stopped dreaming

BENJAMIN FRANKLIN

Having a dream is not trying to believe something regardless of the evidence, dreaming is daring to do something regardless of the consequences. Let your faith run ahead of your mind

JOHN MASON

It is indeed the Dreamers' World and those who reign in life are those who choose to dream. The lot of every man in life is a direct product of the content of his dream. It is what is contained in your dream that determines your placement in this world of dreamers.

As a matter of fact; the only solution to the problems in the world today is dreams that are divinely inspired. A great number of things that have been done in the world in terms of solutions to certain problems at one time or another are direct products of dreams in the hearts of men.

The birth of a great dreamer, Michael Faraday is a great blessing to mankind as a result of the reality of his dream of electric light as a solution to the world of darkness.

The world will never recover from the great dream of Thomas Edison which became a reality in form of the incandescent light bulb after trying to get it done for more than a thousand times.

The great dreamer; Alexander Graham Bell turned his dream of easy communication over a long distance to reality through his invention of the telephone.

Also, Benjamin Franklin became an icon of greatness in the world as a result of the solutions he proffered to some problems by turning his dreams to reality through various inventions.

Isaac Newton; the postulator of the Law of Gravity provided a solution in global scientific development through the reality of his dream.

In his attempt to solve the problem of transportation, Henry Ford invented a new system in the automobile sector. By this, a great number of people can own a car at an affordable price, which had been a dream in his heart for many years before then.

Albert Einstein turned his dream to reality through the invention of the Theory of Relativity, which is a landmark in transforming the scientific world.

There is no doubting the fact that it is a Dreamers' World.

However, there is an underlining factor in the dreams of these great dreamers; and that is **"SOLUTION TO IDENTIFIED PROBLEMS".**

All men known for great achievement are equally recognized to have dreamt of proffering solutions to identified problems. We can see clearly that dreams emerge as a result of prevalent problems that need practical solutions.

Men at one time or another discovered certain problems and in their bid to proffer solutions to those problems, their dreams were born. And as they began to follow after such dreams to bring them to reality, they ended up becoming solution providers in the world.

Indeed, dreamers are solution providers. That is why I have called it the Dreamers' World. Only dreamers are known in this world because their dreams create solutions to the problems of the world and that put them in the world's book of remembrance.

The great dreamer, Benjamin Franklin once said; **"If you want to be remembered after you are dead and rotten, either you do things worth writing or write things worth reading."**

Dreamers are those who have either done things that the world has written about or have written what the world is reading today. In either of the cases, they are making generational impact in the world through their dreams. Great dreams of great dreamers are never fulfilled; they are always transcended.

My discovery in this twenty-first century is that quite a number of people are actually running after wealth. But by virtue of my study of great achievers both in the past and present generations; they are not men who run after wealth, rather, they are men pursuing solutions to identified problems and as they kept following their dreams, wealth began to pursue after them.

Those who are genuinely wealthy do not actually pursue after wealth. They pursue solutions to identified problems through their dreams and as a result wealth pursues after them automatically. Your dream is designed to make you a solution provider. Dreaming is an act of pure imagination, attesting in all people a creative power, which if it were available in waking would make everyman a great success.

The dreamer will always be remembered. If the world must be your possession, you must be a dreamer too, because the world is for dreamers. It is the Dreamers' World.

The truth is that humanity cannot forget its dreamers. It cannot let their ideas fade and die. It lives in them. It knows them as the realities which it shall one day see and know.

Composers, sculptors, painters, poets, prophets and sages; these are the makers of tomorrow. They are the architects of God on earth.

It is not out of place to say that, it is dream that turns ordinary men to extraordinary men; it is dream that turns a weakling to a strong man; it is dream that turns a coward to a bold man and it is dream that turns a pauper to a prosperous man.

Dream is that powerful if it is followed by the dreamer. There is nothing like a dream to create a future. In other words, the future belongs to the dreamers.

Conway Stone, in his book Follow Your Dream, while talking about his country America, he said; ***"The only hope we have is for Anonymous Americans to get in touch with their beliefs and values and follow after their God-given dreams."***

Well, I believe that dream is the only hope we have, if we are to overcome drugs, poverty, the healthcare crisis, welfare, robbery, bribery, overpopulation and apathy, just to name a few. It will not be because of governments or non-profit organizations that have their limitations. NO! It will be because people like you and me, by following our God-given dreams will decide to make a difference in this world. It is dream that empowers men to make a difference in the world. That is why it is the Dreamers' World; that is those who are making a difference in their world.

I believe that as you read this book wherever part of the world you are right now, you have a God-inspired dream and the world is waiting eagerly to see that dream become a realistic solution to her problems.

Friend, your dream has great possibility of becoming a reality, only if you will sit tight to learn all it takes. All you need is a readiness to learn what to do.

It was Isaac Newton who said; ***"If I have been able to see farther than others, it is because I stood on the shoulders of giants."***

Learning is very crucial in turning your dream into reality. No man is a custodian of knowledge. You must be open to learning on a daily basis if fulfillment of your dream is your desire. And most especially, learn from those who have achieved what you dream to achieve.

Alvin Tofler puts it this way; ***"The illiterates of the twenty-first century will not be those who cannot read and write; but those who cannot learn, unlearn and relearn."***

I believe that learning is the missing link between dream and its fulfillment. Those whose dreams have been turned to reality are committed learners of what to do and doers of what they learnt. Leadership and learning are indispensable to each other. The accomplishment of your dream brings you out as a leader; that is why we cannot separate learning from dream and leadership.

Along that line of thought, Henry Ford also noted; "Anyone who stops learning is old, whether at twenty or eighty. Anyone who keeps learning stays young. The greatest thing in life is to keep your mind young."

Therefore, it is not just the Dreamers' World; it is also the Learners' World. It is only the committed learners that will keep ruling the world, because there is power in continuous learning.

WHO IS A DREAMER?

The knowledge of who a dreamer is will help us to identify the source of dreams. I have used different phrases to describe who a dreamer is here;

A dreamer is one who is obsessed with the thought of creating a change.

A dreamer is one who designs a product needed by the people.

A dreamer is one who provides solutions to identified problems.

A dreamer is one who invents things needed by the world

A dreamer is a leader who takes the lead in solving problems.

A dreamer is one who provides services to satisfy the needs of others

A dreamer is one who does things worth writing.

A dreamer is one who writes things worth reading.

A dreamer is one who composes for others to sing.

A dreamer is one who dies for others to live

A dreamer is one who thinks for others to work

A dreamer is one who accomplishes things that the world cannot forget

A dreamer is one who sets the pace for others to follow

A dreamer is a person who influences others to become who God ordained them to be.

I know that you have one or more of the characteristics above. That means you are a dreamer.

Therefore, welcome to your world because, it is the Dreamers' World.

The world is waiting for you just like it waited for Benjamin Franklin, Isaac Newton, Alexander Graham Bell, Michael Faraday, Thomas Edison, Henry Ford, Martin Luther King Jnr, Bill Gates, Ben Carson to mention just a few.

Your dream carries great possibilities; do not play down on its reality. It is the seed of your future greatness; do not toy with its fulfillment. The world belongs to dreamers. If you are one, then it is your world because it is the Dreamers' World.

Hold fast to dreams, for if dreams die, life is a broken winged bird that cannot fly.

LANGSTON HUGHES.

Chapter 2: THE NATURE OF DREAMS

We grow great by dreams. All great men are dreamers. They see things in the soft haze of a spring day or in the red fire of a long winter's evening. Some of us let these great dreams die, but others nourish and protect them and nurse them through bad days till they bring them to the sunshine and light which comes always to those who sincerely hope their dreams will come true.

WOODROW WILSON

The renown that riches or beauty confer is fleeting and frail; mental excellence is a splendid and lasting possession.

SALLUST

The nature of a thing is what determines its value; and its value is what determines its benefits. Dreams are valuable assets; especially, positive and life impacting ones.

As a matter of fact, the world is full of great benefits today because men chose to dream and pursue their dreams.

All progress and advancements in the world today have been made possible by the tireless and persevering pursuit of God-inspired dreams in the hearts of men.

The question then is; what if men refused to dream yesterday, what would have become our world today?

Dreams are valuable assets in creating a future. Today's glory is the future of yesterday's dreams; and the future glory will be the result of today's dreams.

The day man stops dreaming is the day that things begin to go wrong in the world. It is dream that has established great things in our world and greater things yet to come will also be made happen by dream. There can be no accomplishment without a dream. The best you can offer your world is hidden in that dream in you. That is why it is so important for us to understand the nature of dreams and that is what this chapter is out to reveal.

The successful marketing expert, Brian Tracy once said; *"All successful people, men and women are big dreamers. They imagine what their future could be, ideal in every respect, and then they work every day toward their distant vision, goal or purpose."*

That statement reveals that dream is the key to success in every aspect of life.

WHAT IS A DREAM?

Regardless of what it is; a dream is what you want to accomplish in your life. Whatever you are thinking of doing and it takes form in your heart, is your dream.

Whatever is going on in your imagination right now becomes a dream if you allow it to take root. Dream can be anything you want it to be. It depends on what you want to happen in your life.

God has given you the ability to determine what happens in your life by the dream you hold in your heart.

If you want to build a school; it is a dream.

If you want to earn a first and second degree or any academic qualification; it is a dream.

If you want to write a book; it is a dream.

If you want to sing as an artiste; it is a dream.

If you want to start a business; it is a dream.

If you want to establish a ministry when you have a divine call, it is a dream.

If you want to shed weight; it is a dream.

If you want to create wealth, it is a dream.

No matter what it is that you want to do in life; it is a dream. I will put it this way:

Anything; and I mean, anything, that you want to accomplish in your life becomes your dream.

However, the main source of dream is the heart. Dream is a product of wisdom and the heart is the seat of wisdom.

Vines Expository Dictionary of Old and New Testament Words (W.E. Vine, Edited by F. F. Bruce, Fleming H. Revell Co. Old Tappan, N.J., 1981) defines heart as man's entire mental and moral activity, both the rational and the emotional elements.

The Greek word for heart in the New Testament is Kardia and it denotes the seat of physical life, the seat of moral nature and spiritual life, the desires, the affections, the perceptions, the thoughts, the understanding, the reasoning powers, the imagination, conscience, the intentions and the will.

The heart, in its moral significance in the Old Testament includes the emotions, the reason and the will. The heart refers to the human brain. It is the place where "thinking" occurs.

Therefore, heart is that which is central! Your core.... Your inner being. It is the central controlling system for all thinking, reasoning and feeling activities.

In Proverbs 4:23, King Solomon admonished and said;

Keep thy heart with all diligence; for out of it are the issues of life.

Also, in Proverbs 23:7, he said;

For as he thinketh in his heart, so is he: Eat and drink, saith he to thee; but his heart is not with thee"

The heart of man is the seat of wisdom where dreams emanate from. Your heart is the factory where your dreams are manufactured.

The great author, Mark Victor Hansen said; **"Thoughts and ideas are the source of all** *wealth, success, material gain, all great discoveries, inventions and achievements".*

The issues of life that come from the heart are dreams.

1 Peter 1:13;

Wherefore gird up the loins of your mind, be sober, and hope to the end for the grace that is to be brought unto you at the revelation of Jesus Christ;

And in Matthew 12:34, Jesus said;

...for out of the abundance of the heart the mouth speaketh.

The understanding of this truth is pivotal, because whatever you allow to stay in your heart becomes your dream and that is what you will carry out.

Please note that what you do not think about in your heart cannot happen in your life.

And it is what you think about continuously that determines where you will end up. Your life will always move in the direction of your most dominant thought.

Your dream has its source in your heart, that is, what you are thinking about. Big thinking precedes great achievement and the size of your success will depend on the size of your dream. Also, dream can be viewed as reflections of what we value and believe. Dreams proceed from Values and Beliefs.

However, Beliefs and Values are formed by our continual thinking. By examining what we believe, by examining what we want to base our lives on, and by continually thinking about these beliefs, our Beliefs and Values are shaped. And of course you know that the predominant function of the heart is thinking. That is why it is impossible to separate dreams from thoughts. Dreams are formed by thoughts.

In order to succeed, man must first determine which things in life are most valuable to him. He must determine his feeling about such things as patriotism, pride, love, freedom, excellence, ownership and tolerance. Without a value system we can never move forward, because, we may be trading without increasing our potential for success. Our value system is what determines our thinking and dream patterns.

The great philosopher William James noted; ***"If you can change your mind, you can change your life."***

In other words, the results you are getting will remain the same if what you are thinking remains unchanged. The heart of man is so powerful that whatever is programmed into it as a result of continual and consistent thinking, will eventually take its practical form in reality.

It has been proven scientifically that the subconscious mind is the control room of human life. Whatever thought is programmed into it, the reality will automatically be created. Your subconscious mind creates your reality based on a number of messages you send to it. Some of these messages are the pictures and images that you visualize and send to your subconscious mind. It then picks up this creative visualization or picture and begins to create what it sees whether positive or negative.

The reason is because, people are basically visual as designed by God. We have pictures in our head of what we think is true about the world; and physically, emotionally, mentally, spiritually, and by our actions, we move towards these pictures. We live out what we believe in our mind.

Another basic principle of life is that, if we want to change our lives, we have to change the pictures we have in our heads. If we change the pictures in our heads, we will physically, emotionally, mentally, spiritually and by our actions move towards those new pictures.

It is the information in our hearts that determines our thoughts, it is our thoughts that determine our dreams; and it is our dreams that determine our accomplishments in life.

Therefore, it is our most noble duties to constantly feed our hearts with the right information through the book of wisdom (the Bible), anointed materials like books and tapes, biographies of great dreamers and so on. Information from these can help to shape our dreams for positive impact.

Bill Gates, the founder of Microsoft Empire and a multimillionaire once said; "I really had a lot of dreams when I was a kid, and I think a great deal of that grew out of the fact that I had a chance to read a lot."

From that statement made by Bill Gates, it is very clear that reading formed a major part of what brought about his success in the business world. So, it is your personal responsibility to program your thoughts well so as to generate dreams that will bring the best of God out of your life.

Sometimes ago, I was reading one of the books written by Dr. David Yonggi Cho who is the pastor of the largest church in the world situated in South Korea and I discovered that God is interested in establishing what we dream. The Spirit of God is the one that actually puts dreams into the hearts of men.

Please, read what Dr. David Yonggi Cho said about the place of dreaming in accomplishing great things in life; *"A dream (or vision) is the basic material the Holy Spirit uses to build anything for you. When you don't have a dream (or vision), you don't produce anything.*

Dreaming seems foolish to the rational mind, and I would agree, if dreaming is done without a goal. But when you establish a goal and begin to dream for that goal, that dream becomes creative. The Holy Spirit uses it to bring the future to the present. If you don't have a dream, you will never reach that goal. I am constantly living in the world of God-given dreams. Keep on dreaming. You are going to grow only as big as your dream".

This great man ascended the throne of greatness by his dream. Although God called him into preaching and pastoral ministry and he is heavily anointed by God for his assignment, the calling and the anointing were not the major factors to the success he accomplished; his ability to dream; to create a mental picture of the kind of future he desired was the key according to his personal testimony as we have discovered from his statements above.

That simply means that no matter what kind of a person you are, what race you are from, what background you have, what nation you come from, or what kind of assignment God has given to you on earth; as long as you desire to succeed in this life, you must have a dream. This is because; you can only create your future from your future, not from your past. You can only create a future by seeing into the future, not by holding onto the past.

If God is the force behind your dream, it must be a big one because God is a big God and He cannot accomplish anything less than big things.

Let God be your motivator so that He will be the driving force for your dream in life. Dreams often flounder when we neglect to make God our partner and ask for His advice in the pursuit of them.

You cannot afford to remain small in your thought pattern. Think big and dream great dreams as you make God your dream partner.

Remember what Solomon said in Proverbs 23:7;

...as he thinketh in his heart, so is he....

If great accomplishment is your desire, then developing a great dream must be your responsibility. God expects you to dream big and then surrender your dream to Him for His help to bring it to reality. You are limited only by your dream because your imagination has the capacity to achieve anything in life.

CREATING THE ACTUAL PICTURE OF YOUR DREAM

In her book Your Invisible Power, Genevieve Behrend said; **"Try to remember that the** *picture you think, feel and see is reflected into the Universal Mind, and by the natural law of reciprocal action must return to you in either spiritual or physical form."* This means pictures are formed by your thought pattern and this eventually transforms into your dream in real life. There are pictures your have seen in a particular place many years ago that makes you remember what happened then. That is how powerful pictures can be.

When you begin to create the actual pictures of your dream and look at the pictures regularly, you will begin to move towards bringing those pictures into realities.

Bob Proctor, when describing the Law of Attraction said; **"Everything coming into your life, you** *are attracting into your life. And it is attracted to you by virtue of the images (pictures) you are holding in your mind. Whatever is going on in your mind, you are attracting to you."*

If you create the actual pictures of your dream, those pictures will become your realities. Devising a new language of pictures may be precisely what we need to tackle the world's biggest challenges. And your dream is meant to be a solution to the world's present and future challenges. That means, creating the actual picture of your dream is what makes you a practical dreamer in this Dreamers' World.

I believe it is time you begin to paint the actual picture of that dream you have. If your dream is to build a global business that will solve problems, then get the actual pictures of the network of branches that your company will have in different parts of the world and every other thing that pertains to that company, and then put it where you can see it clearly everyday.

The more you see it everyday, the more passionate you become in moving towards it. It is not enough to talk about it; it is very important that you paint it in pictures.

And if you have been there in the mind, automatically, you will go there in the body. In other words, if you have the picture, the blueprint or master plan in your mind, you will naturally begin to walk practically with that picture in real life.

Let me share my experience with you. A few years ago, I needed a laptop for my work. After reading the book Tough Times Never Last, But Tough People Do by Robert Schuller, I discovered that I could get anything I wanted in life only if I could picture it. Then I went to buy a laptop bag with the picture of a Dell Latitude laptop in the bag. At that time, I did not have the cash to buy the laptop, but I cut the picture and I took it with me in my pocket everywhere I went. Also, I went to work every morning with the bag as if I already had my laptop. It was not long when I started doing that that an opportunity opened up for me to get the money for the laptop. The moment the cash came, I gave it to someone who knew about laptop to get me the best based on the amount I gave him. Surprisingly, the person bought the exact type of laptop in the picture I was carrying about, yet I did not give him any specification, neither did he have any idea of the picture I was carrying about. That means the picture I had both in my mind and in my hand attracted to me the exact physical equivalent. That is how powerful dreams with visualization can be.

Today, I have a series of pictures with me that represent my dreams and many of them have already become tangible products in my life. Dreaming with actual picture is the most powerful key to speedy accomplishments in life.

It is very important to dream big. A big dream is one that has the capacity of global influence and a generational lifespan. A big dream is the one that you cannot accomplish in your lifetime. It will keep on speaking after you are gone. In other words big or great dream will continue to generate impact in the lives of generations after you. That is a big dream. If you have a dream that you can accomplish in your lifetime, it is too small a dream and when you limit what you think you can do, you have limited what you can accomplish.

The man Walt Disney dreamed of a place where families all over the United States could come and spend quality time having fun. That gave birth to DISNEYLAND. This has put smiles on the faces of families all around America today.

Mr. Disney was turned down 302 times before he got financing for his dream of creating the **"Happiest Place on Earth."**

He was a man in touch with his dream as a great dreamer and he refused to give up until he accomplished the content of his dream.

No matter what your dream is, it has a great possibility to become a reality if you hold on to it. The world is in the need of positive dreamers like Abraham Lincoln, Martin Luther King Jnr, Benjamin Franklin, Isaac Newton, Michael Faraday, David Oyedepo, Oral Robert, others and you, the reader of this book.

Now my admonition to you is that you dream big and positive dreams. It does not really matter what the dream is, as long as it is big and positive, it has the ability to bring creative impact to the world. Also, make God your dream partner because if you take God out of the picture of your dream, it does not have the certainty of being fulfilled.

However, what are the elements and characteristics of dreams, especially big and positive dreams?

DREAM AIDS IN FULFILLING DIVINE PURPOSE

Man is a product of divine purpose. As you are going to discover in chapter 4 of this book, there is no man on earth today without a reason in God's mind before he was created. But no matter what God has created you to do on earth, you must have big and positive dreams for you to be able to fulfill that purpose.

Remember, you are living on earth where you are to carry out your heaven ordained purpose which is designed by God to bring impact to the people. That is why you must have dreams that will enhance your impact on earth. You must be a dream partner with God in order to affect your world with your God-given purpose. Your dream is like a vision without which you cannot fulfill your purpose. (Proverbs 29:18)

DREAM CREATES A FUTURE

The dreams of yesterday are the realities of today and the dreams of today will be the realities of tomorrow. It is dream that creates the future you and I are expecting. That means, if you don't have any dream today, there is no future to expect.

Begin to dream now and make sure you put your dream on paper so that you can work it out as you turn it to reality. It is dreams that give life and provide hope for the future.

DREAM CREATES DESIRED CHANGE

If you do not want to remain on a spot for years, you need to have a dream so as to create the change you desire. If you have a dream of earning a degree today and you pursue it, at the end of four years of study in the university, your desired change will have been realized by the fulfillment of that dream.

If you are poor now and you have a dream of becoming wealthy, as you pursue that dream, you will attain your change of status from poverty to prosperity.

DREAM BRINGS ONE INTO GREATNESS

I love the story of Farrah Gray, a very young black American guy as I read from his book a few years ago. This young chap came from a very poor background; the family sometimes could not afford to pay rent and they all had to sleep outside in the car until they were able to pay up the rent. But in the midst of all those discomforts as it were, this boy caught a dream of becoming a wealthy man by creating his own business. He followed his dream at age seven and by the time he was fifteen years old, he was already a millionaire and was invited for a special meeting in White house where he had a commendation with a hand shake with the then president of United States of America, Mr. Bill Clinton.

Also he was invited to sit on the Boards of Directors of great companies in America. It was his dream that took him from poverty to wealth and he became a great and positive influence in the business world, an icon and a model to many young people in the world.

Your own dream can also bring you to such great level of greatness.

DREAM BRINGS PROSPERITY AND LASTING WEALTH

When you give yourself to a dream of service to humanity, the fulfillment of that dream will bring you into wealth.

Bill Gates' dream has always been to create a I.T. products that will provide business solutions at a very cheap cost for people in the world and by it, he founded Microsoft Corporation in 1985. Today Bill Gates is rated as one of the richest men in the world as he is worth over fifty billion US Dollar.

What if Bill Gates did not dream of solving business problems for mankind? He might not have got to that level of wealth today.

DREAM BRINGS GLOBAL INFLUENCE AND RECOGNITION

All the dreamers I have talked about so far in this book are international figures who are well known for their great accomplishments. It was their dreams of yesterday that brought them into global recognition today. Dream has the capacity of making you a global celebrity.

There is no way you will talk about transformations in the university education without mentioning names of great dreamers like Dr. Oral Robert, US (Oral Robert University), Dr. David Oyedepo, Nigeria (Covenant University and Landmark University), Dr. Mensa Otabil, Ghana (Central Africa University) et cetera. These men have become icons in the international community as a result of their dreams.

Friend, your dream can do the same for you because there is no respect of persons with God. If you can do what they did, then you can get the kind of result they got. You can even do better than they have done if you will learn from them and improve upon what they have accomplished.

Anthony Robins that once; *"If anyone can do anything in the world, you can do too."*

It is time for your own manifestation through your dream; it is your dream that manifests you to your world. The world is waiting for your own accomplishment which will bring advancement to it. This will happen by your dream.

Thought is the fountain of action, life and manifestation; make the fountain pure, and all will be pure. All that man achieves and all that he fails to achieve is the direct result of his thoughts. As he thinks, so he is, as he continues to think, so re remains.

JAMES ALLEN

Chapter 3: DREAMS ARE MENTAL PROJECTIONS

Every thought of form held in thinking substance, causes the creation of the form, but always, or at least, generally, along the lines of growth and action already established

WALLACE D. WATTLES

Your mental picture determines your actual future and you cannot feature in a future you have not pictured

DAVID OYEDEPO

Make your brain work. It will sweat; but make it work. It will improve. It will develop until you become a wonder to those around you.

E.W. KENYON

I will like to open this chapter by illustrating the processes involved in developing a dream using the story of the great man; father Abraham, as recorded in the Bible.

Genesis 13:14-15;

And the LORD said unto Abram, after that Lot was separated from him, Lift up now thine eyes, and look from the place where thou art northward, and southward, and eastward, and westward:

For ALL THE LAND WHICH THOU SEEST, TO THEE WILL I GIVE IT, AND TO THY SEED FOR EVER.

Here God spoke to Abraham to take responsibility for creating his future by developing a dream. Whatever he could see became his dream and God would give it to him as long as he could see it.

Whatever Abraham desires, all he needed to do was to look and see them, and then all he could see would become his possessions.

But I believe that God wanted Abraham to see with his inner eyes, not just the physical. There was no way he could have seen everything in the four dimensions of the earth all at once with his physical eyes.

After a very deep thought on that statement of God to Abraham, I concluded that another kind of eyes are needed to see all those things, and that must be the inner eyes. This is where the power of mental projection was established.

As creatures of God, we are expected to learn how to project into the future and form a picture of what we desire to see physically accomplished in our lives; because God has made us to be creators of our own realities.

Therefore, dream is simply the act of mentally projecting into the future. If your actions are being dictated by your present physical environment, then you don't have a dream.

The reason why people are poor and remain in poverty is because, they hang the picture of poverty in their heart and as long as that picture remains there, prosperity is not in view for them. What you constantly view is what is in view for you.

It is your mental projection that gives motion to your life. The picture in your heart is what dictates your actions in life. Your destiny is determined by your mental picture. That mental picture is your dream. If you have a mental picture of poverty, you will reflect that picture in your physical life. And when you change that picture in your mental faculty to wealth, nothing can stop you from becoming wealthy irrespective of your background, education or the part of the world you came from.

The great man of God, Kenneth Copeland puts it this way; *"Destiny is not built overnight. It is not what you thought once or twice that got you where you are today. It's what you've thought over and over again. Those inner images are created by repetition and repetition takes time."*

Do not be surprised that on a daily basis you are building your destiny, whether positively or negatively by your mental projections. Whatever has not passed through your mind cannot happen in your life. But once a thought comes in and you open up your heart to it, whether positive or negative, it becomes an inner image and then it forms the basis upon which you live.

This book is written to help you know how to create a great future by learning how to create great and positive mental projections with which your future can be secured.

However, in this chapter, I will share with you on how to project positively into your future by learning from the lives of great men who have accomplished great things through their dreams.

Remember that your ability to learn from others is what determines the speed you will gain in fulfilling your own destiny.

Napoleon Bonaparte said; **"Great men are meteors designed to burn so that the earth may be lightened."**

When we choose to learn from others, we are ready to experience a turnaround in our own lives.

THEY ALL HAD DREAMS

Here, I will show by practical examples and real life story of some great dreamers who are people with great mental projections, though they were poor at the beginning, their dreams took them to wealth and greatness. That is what God wants for you too.

COSMAS MADUKA lost his father at the age of four, and as a result of that his education was cut short. At a very young age, he became an automobile apprentice in his uncle's automobile parts business in Ebute-Metta area of Lagos Nigeria.

He worked for his uncle for seven years before starting his own business in 1975. Cosmas' uncle provided him with 200 Naira in capital with which he used to start his own auto parts business in Nnewi. He did not allow the unfortunate circumstances surrounding him to hinder his drive for success, because he had a dream for the future.

Today, he is the CEO of Coscharis Group, with about 10 subsidiaries and branches in Nigeria and abroad.

In the Nigerian automobile market, the name Coscharis is quite prominent. Coscharis motors specializes in the sale of BMW and Landrover; the company is in partnership with BMW of Germany. It was a dream come true for Maduka to be the sole representative of BMW in Nigeria because he personally has a penchant for BMW cars.

His business is presently worth over 15 billion Naira and they engage in socially responsible projects such as the donation of a Law Lecture Theater in University of Nigeria, Enugu campus and the construction of roads in his hometown of Nnewi. It is also worthy to note that he has been given an honorary doctorate degree of Science by The University of Nigeria, Nsukka.

He is the President of the Nigerian Table Tennis Federation; the Vice President of the Nigeria-Japan Association. In addition, is a member of Electric Power Reform Implementation Committee in Nigeria, a Trustee Board Member of the Human Development Fund of the United Nations Development Program. He has attended various training program within and outside the country on all business related fields. This is what a dream can turn a man without secondary and university education into.

While delivering a lecture on Business & Economy syndicate session at the 2010 Excellence In Leadership Conference organized by Daystar

Christian Centre in November 2010, I heard Mr. Maduka made this profound statements among others; "Of course, my father's death affected my education. There are things that will happen to you and you may think that is the end of the world. But I must tell you that there are some of us who have turned our difficulties into dividends and problems into opportunities. I believe that if I had gone to school, I would have made a first class because I have what it takes to make it."

He said further; *"The most important thing in life is to focus on what you have, not on what you do not have. Enduring success is achieved by a clear vision and sound management strategies. Your desire to succeed must be greater than your fear to fail and dream is the major key to building a great business".*

He is a great dreamer who knows what it takes to turn a dream into reality.

SAM WALTON, a great dreamer and founder of Sam's Club and Wal-Mart, the world's largest general retail chain of valued priced variety stores. Although he had setbacks because his first and second variety stores went bankrupt, yet Mr. Walton held on to his dream knowing that dreams provided hope for the future.

During his time at the university, he worked odd jobs to help feed and support himself. He graduated with a degree in economics and was known as an honorable, scholarly student.

With his degree, Sam Walton joined the management team of JC Penny in Des Moines, Iowa, only three days after graduation. Having served with the ROTC in college, Walton anticipated military service when World War II began in 1942. Walton resigned his position and worked at the DuPont munitions plant awaiting his call to duty. It was in this plant that he met Helen Robson, his future wife. They met in April of 1942 and married in February of 1943. Shortly thereafter, Walton left with the military to serve with the Intelligence Corps where he eventually became a captain.

Walton had a stint with the military till 1945; he left and decided to open his own department stores. His father-in-law loaned him the initial $20,000 added to the $5,000 to start his first store, a Ben Franklin franchise variety store, in Arkansas.

Sam Walton wanted to focus on providing a wide range of goods at discounted prices to the consumer and keep his stores opened longer than his competitors, even during the Christmas season. His lower-priced strategies allowed him to drive up sales and negotiate lower prices on purchases with his wholesalers. A combination of his location and price strategies made him a top seller in the chain in the six-state region of the franchise market.

Walton is best known for starting the chain "Wal-Mart" which first opened in 1962 in Bentonville, Arkansas. He transferred his philosophies from his Ben Franklin stores to his own brand stores in the process and worked hard to help bring a large variety of products and low prices to his customers throughout his career. He remained dedicated to keeping Wal-Mart involved in local activities by allowing charities to hold bake sales on his property as well as providing scholarships to high school graduates from local schools.

As a result of his accomplishments, Sam Walton eventually received the Presidential Medal of Freedom from the U.S President, George H. W. Bush in 1992. Also, he reached the ranks of the richest man in the U.S from 1985 until 1988. Walton passed away on April 6, 1992 and left his business to his wife and children who became the primary shareholders of the company keeping the great dream on till date.

By 2001, Wal-Mart had over 4500 stores worldwide. Also, it was the largest company in the world listed in Fortune 500 in 2007, 2008 and 2010. As at 2013 Fortune Global 500 list, Wal-Mart is the biggest private employer in the world with over two million, two hundred employees, and is the largest retailer in the world with over 8,970 stores globally.

Friend, no matter the financial challenges you may have, keep your dream alive because it has great possibilities. Just hang on one more time as Mr. Walton did, and you will also triumph at the end.

SUNNY OBAZU OJEAGBASE, the Publisher, Success Digest; Complete Football; Complete Sports and Sports Souvenir had no university or polytechnic education, but through diligent personal development, resoluteness and faith in God, built one of the most thriving publishing businesses in Nigeria.

As a result of his passion for people, he has a mission to equip budding entrepreneurs with tools they needed to create wealth, add value to society and live their dreams as he teaches the tremendous benefits that always come with a commitment to personal development.

Before his breakthrough, he was miserable, desperate and he needed help. This led him to commit his life to God and began a journey of personal discovery; he began to read the Bible which led to the turning point in his life.

In 1974, he read a book titled **"The Seven Laws of Success"** by W. Herbert Armstrong and there he discovered the secrets that helped him to change the course of his life. One of the major things he discovered was the need to find one's passion and build ones career or business around it. He looked inward and found out that he had a deep desire for journalism and sports. He then thought of what he could do that would combine both interests. He decided to walk that path and that led him into a most adventurous, challenging and successful journey.

Before then, all he had as educational qualification was a Primary six Leaving School Certificate, but having discovered his passion, he registered for GCE where he had just two papers. Then he put in for home study course in Journalism and pursued his sports journalism career tenaciously. He worked with some publishing houses and rose to the position of a Sports Editor.

In 1983, having visited one of his mentors, he saw two books with him Think and Grow Rich and Success Through a Positive Mental Attitude by

Napoleon Hill and W. Clement Stone which he requested to read.

From these books, he discovered that to be successful, you need to provide a quality service to people in the proportion to the size of the wealth you desire. That spurred him into entrepreneurship as he started sports publishing business with the name Complete Communications Limited (CCL), is a major publishing outfit in the field of sports in Nigeria today. Also, he started an NGO with his wife Esther, named Success Attitude Development Centre (SADC) with a mission to raise and nurture entrepreneurs whose success in business will be driven by the fear of God.

Sunny, was noted for his passion for books as he once said; *"The story of my life would have been different if it were not for the books I have been privileged to read."*

MICHAEL FRIDAY was a studio boy in a church in Abuja Nigeria, but he had a dream of greatness in the field of IT. He decided to resign from being a studio boy in order to pursue the future of greatness he had seen.

Strikingly, Friday's humble beginning meant that he had to face the harsh reality of having to drop out of the Yaba College of Technology (Nigeria) at a point due to financial constraints. But he overcame that vicissitude, and today, he not only has a master's degree in Information Technology from Liverpool University, England, he sits atop an engineering concern Vivid Vision Global Resources that produces laptops, navigators, and flash drives.

Among his numerous inventions are a flash drive of 16 and 32 gigabytes. He says, **"They are the largest in the market today. Besides being immune to virus, it is manufactured from copper wire and has a microchip technology, which makes the storage of data as fast as the speed of light".**

There is also the GPRS navigator, a dual purpose electronic product combining the functions of a sophisticated mobile phone. Having realized that the theft of laptops in Nigeria is on the rise, Friday went into the development of Vivid Laptops, fully made and configured for the Nigerian environment.

The climax of his inventions is the 2.4 litre engine car, which is still Work in progress. He says the car, when eventually unveiled, will use no fuel. The car, according to Friday, will use just hydraulic brake fluid and engine oil and a day-to-day back up charging of the in-built module to enable it to travel for 2,000 miles at the touch of a button.

Michael was able to achieve all these at the age of twenty-nine, because he had a dream, having discovered his place of God's calling in life. This young Nigerian now has branches of his company in China and Nigeria. Also, he has won both National and International Awards. His dream has transformed his life positively.

Friend, I believe that, there is nothing you cannot accomplish if you have a dream and are passionate enough to pursue it, no matter your age.

Your fulfillment in life is a function of your dream which comes by your mental projection. If all these men can find success in life through their dreams, you too can. You might not even look like someone who can become great in life; relax, the men whose stories I have shared with you did not look like those who could be known in their communities, but today they are known world wide by virtue of the accomplishment of their dreams.

If you will have a dream and follow that dream, you will become a success and a blessing to your generation.

You can be the designer of your life or the victim of your circumstances; it's up to you. Create you own success through a positive mental projection and hold fast to it with persistence, perseverance and patience until it becomes a reality.

PART TWO

FULFILLING YOUR DREAM

In this section, I will be showing you seven-proven and failure-proof strategic steps to take to fulfill your dream. These steps, if followed accordingly, are sure to give a speedy accomplishment to your dream in life.

The greatest man who ever lived on earth, Jesus Christ our Lord made use of these steps and He left us an example so that we can fulfill our own God-given dreams on earth.

However, these steps place a great demand on you. They clearly reveal to us that, dream does not fulfill itself. These steps are like the driver that drives the vehicle of your dream to the land of fulfillment.

As a matter of fact, these steps are divine principles commanded by God for us to take in order to fulfill our dreams in life.

As you put these steps into practical use, you cannot fail to have your dream come true.

Nevertheless, these steps are only recommended for only those who have taken time to read the first three chapters of this book and are now ready to develop a dream for their lives. They will only produce for the serious dreamers, not just an individual who is not ready to achieve anything in life.

I know that you have a dream because from my teachings and illustrations, you can see that only through dreams can greatness be attained in life.

So you are the one I am presenting these seven success-proven strategic steps to.

I want to read about your own success very soon as you fulfill your own God-given dream in life.

No matter your age right now, the revelations I have share in the next chapters have the power to transform your life as you get yourself committed to the practice of the strategic, God-ordained success principles.

Chapter 4: DISCOVER YOUR PURPOSE

The tragedy of life is that too many people will die with their music still unplayed.

OLIVER WENDEL HOLMES

There is a reason why you are here. And the best way to self-fulfillment, the best way to happiness, is to get in touch with that reason and align your actions and habits with that purpose.

CONWAY STONE

Most people who set out to make a change or improvement in their lives never do so because they do not understand the power of 'WHY.'

KACPER M. POSTAWSKI

The preliminary point in the race of life is to discover the purpose for which we are given life. Man is a creature of purpose, he is not a biological accident; neither is he a result of happenstance. Every man on earth today exists for a peculiar purpose. The purpose for which man was created is the reason why he is on earth.

Also, purpose is peculiar, because no two men have the same purpose. Two men can have a similar assignment, but the purpose for which God created each one is peculiar to each one. Your purpose is the specific song you are born to sing, but my question to you is; Are you singing the song you were sent to this earth to sing?

The most important principle of life is that: **"Nothing exists without a Purpose".**

The subject of purpose is so important and dream is one of the most powerful tools for fulfillment of man's purpose on earth. In other words, your dream is a reflection of your purpose in life. What you are dreaming of accomplishing now is a revelation of the reason why God has created you.

You were put on Earth to fulfill a specific purpose; your responsibility is to discover it and achieve it. That means you must be able to find out the reason why God has created you before you can fulfill it. Much of the time, people expend too much effort working on the 'how' whereas what they really need to focus on is the **'*why.*'**

If you don't have a strong enough reason, you will not find out what you need to know, you will not do the things you need to do, when you need to do them. I believe moving towards a worthy purpose will provide the greatest fulfillment.

Fulfillment of destiny is not possible without a discovery of purpose. You have been given the responsibility to find out your own peculiar purpose for life.

Your purpose is original because it is meant for you only to fulfill on earth. Nobody can do what you were created to do.

Dr. Myles Munroe, a world renowned teacher of the subject of purpose puts it this way; **"When purpose is not known, abuse is inevitable."**

This simply means that you will use your life abnormally if you do not know the purpose for which God gave it to you.

He said further; **"It is better to be dead and not know life than to be alive and not know why."**

The reason is because; it is what God has created you for that will be made to happen in your life. But if you don't know it, you cannot work it to reality. Therefore, your purpose and your dream are inseparable. It is your purpose that dictates your dream or to say it in another way; Your Purpose Is The Source Of Your Dream.

I want to strongly admonish you that you take out time to discover your purpose before you begin to develop your dream. It is your discovered purpose that will dictate your values and beliefs which becomes the source of your dream.

Anthony Robbins said; ***"Human beings are capable of incredible things. If we have a big enough REASON to do something, we'll go to the greatest lengths to get it done."***

You do not know how powerful you are until you discover the reason why you are created by God, your Manufacturer.

What is purpose?

Purpose can be defined as an intention, an aim or a function of something; a reason for doing something. It is the original intention for creation and the reason why a thing was made.

In other words, your purpose is the original intention of God for creating you. Before you were created, God had an intention of what He wanted you to do and then He created you to carry out that intention.

Therefore, your purpose on earth is the divine plan of God for you, which is permanent and cannot change. That means your purpose was established before your formation. You are not a biological accident. You did not just exist. You are on a divine mission on earth with a purpose to fulfill.

The most secure place in the world is not in any country; whether developed, developing or underdeveloped, rather it is in the WILL (purpose) of God. If you align your plan with His purpose, you will reach the pinnacle of your dream.

Purpose And Identity

Your purpose is why you were created by God; your identity is who you are in God. It is the knowledge of 'who' you are that lends credence to the knowledge of 'why' you are.

Who' you are is your identity; 'why' you are is your purpose.

You cannot separate one from the other. The knowledge of who you are has a lot to do with how you think about yourself; and your thinking about yourself will affect your dream which will ultimately determine your reality.

You need to understand that, there is nothing as important in your life as your mental attitude towards yourself - what you think of yourself, the model which you hold of yourself and your possibilities.

It is the knowledge of who you are that dictates your mental attitude toward yourself and that mental attitude will dictate how you relate with your creator who is the source of your purpose.

Therefore, it is not out of place to conclude that; if you are ignorant of who you are, you are definitely ignorant of who God is. And since you are ignorant of who God is, you will be ignorant of His purpose for your life. Then having a positive dream that will make you a person of impact in the world will be impossible.

All men of exploits are men with deep knowledge of their creator. And that helps them to have the knowledge of who they are which leads to their knowledge of 'why' they were created and then from their knowledge of their purpose they had dreams that have made them great in life.

The major truth of life is that, you can not be truly successful until you truly know yourself.

Now, my question to you is; WHO ARE YOU?

Until you answer this question, you cannot effectively answer the question of 'why' you exist. Once you are able to answer this question, you are on the way to fulfilling your dream in life. The best place to begin the search for the knowledge of who you are is to look into your Manufacturer's manual which is the Bible.

You are not a candidate for successful accomplishment in life if you separate your life from the Word of God packaged in the Bible.

Joshua 1:8;

This Book of the Law shall not depart from your mouth, but you shall meditate in it day and night, that you may observe to do according to all that is written in it. For then you will make your way prosperous, and then you will have good success.

You can only make your way prosperous and obtain good success through your knowledge of God which is available to you as you study the Word. When you take the time to study the lives of successful men in the past and present generations; you will discover how frequently they make reference to the Bible.

I believe that as a student of life's issues, the names of men like Abraham Lincoln, Benjamin Franklin, Michael Faraday, Martin Luther King Jnr, Helen Keller, David Oyedepo, Joyce Meyer, Myles Munroe, John C. Maxwell, etc. will come readily to your mind.

However, you will also discover that their major secrets of success and fulfillment in life are based on Biblical teachings. I am convinced of that, because I have taken the time over the years to study about many of them and how they were able to accomplish great things on earth. Pick up your Bible to find out who you are and then you can discover your purpose in life which will determine your dream. Don't forget; if you don't know 'who' you are, you will be ignorant of 'why' you are. And you cannot have a God given dream which will lead to your success in life.

TYPES OF SIGHT

Insight

This is the ability to see into the depth of a situation. Insight is synonymous with intuition which means inner teacher and it also means perspective. Insight is a combination of experience, reasoning, views and sensitivity to the voice of your inner man within you. You have to listen to the voice within. You have to learn how to turn down the volume of the voice outside and turn on the volume of the voice of your inner man. This voice tells you who you are and what can happen in your life.

Foresight

This is the ability to see into the future. It is about where you are going; your destination and your determination to get there. Foresight is the ability to see what has not happened in your mind (or spirit) and being ready to create them in the physical realm. That is exactly what vision is. To have foresight is to have a vision. Foresight is the type of sight that helps you see way down the road and believe in the possibility of what you see.

You must have both insight and foresight and be able to combine the two to form a dream and then you must believe in the possibility of your dream.

Insight mixed with foresight gives you the key for tapping into the power of dream for exploits.

Mission Statement

Now that you understand what purpose means, the power of identity, the place of vision, the next thing is to develop a Mission Statement.

I defined a Mission Statement as one statement that describes what you want to accomplish in life. It is just one statement, though it could be a combination of sentences in form of compound or complex sentence, but it is just a statement describing what you stand for in life.

Susan Ward, a Management Expert, defines Mission Statement as a brief description of a company's fundamental purpose both for those in the organization and for the public.

Your Mission Statement must be in line with your dream. I know that your dream has the possibility of becoming a reality, but you need to reduce the details of that dream into one statement called a ***"Mission Statement"***.

What is your dream in life? Use that dream to develop a Mission Statement that will give shape and meaning to your life as you read this statement to yourself with passion everyday. You must discover your purpose, discover who you are, have a vision and develop a Mission Statement.

Chapter 5: DISCOVER AND RELEASE YOUR POTENTIAL

"Potential is never what you have done; it is always what you could do but you haven't done yet"

MYLES MUNROE

"Man has been programmed by God to do only according to what he knows. But he has been given the ability to program himself to do more daily by knowing more daily as he learns more daily"

SUNDAY A. EZEKIEL

"It is necessary that we make the right choices, find out what our talents and

abilities are and have them properly trained and fitted to achieve the desired end"

E.W. KENYON

The next strategic point to understand in the pursuit of your dream in life is your potential. You cannot separate your potential from the fulfillment of your dream, just as you cannot separate a man from a woman to have a baby.

In other words potential and dream are inseparable. The vision of what can happen through you cannot be separated from the ability of God in you in the form of gifts and talents. What you can do springs from the knowledge of the resources that you have to do it. Everyman on earth is endowed by God with resources according to each one's ability.

In the greatest book of success on earth, the Bible, Jesus revealed this truth in a parable in Matthew 25:14-15;

For the kingdom of heaven is as a man travelling into a far country, who called his own servants, and delivered unto them his goods.

And unto one he gave five talents, to another two, and to another one; to EVERY MAN ACCORDING TO HIS SEVERAL ABILITY; and straightway took his journey.

That parable reveals that every creature of God is divinely endowed according to what each one has capacity to handle.

That talent, gift or ability is what is known as potential. It is everyone's responsibility to discover his potential; and not only to discover them but to harness them to fulfill his dreams in life.

The truth is that, potential is given by God for the accomplishment of our dreams. In other words, if you don't discover your potential and harness it properly, there is the possibility of not achieving the object of your dream in life.

We all possess the ability to reach the top of our own unique 'Mount Everest'. I've learned that true success is not so much about being talented as it is about what you do with that talent. Even though God has given you potential in form of talent; the purpose of those gifts is to fulfill your God-given dream, vision and purpose in life.

What is potential?

Dr Myles Munroe defined potential as unexposed ability, reserved power, untapped strength, capped capabilities, unused success, dormant gifts, hidden talents and latent power.

Potential is what you can do that you haven't done; where you can go that you haven't gone; who you can be that you are yet to be; how far you can reach that you haven't yet reached; what you can see that you haven't yet seen; what you can accomplish that you haven't yet accomplished.

In other words, it doesn't matter what you have done before now, there are still things that you can do that is hidden in you. You need to understand that your dream is related to your potential. If you can dream anything, that is the evidence that you can do it. The dream in your heart now, no matter how impossible it may appear, it can be done because in as much as you can dream it you can do it.

Potential is the sum total of who you are that you are yet to reveal. Your potential is what God deposited in you that can change your world.

The best way to discover your full potential is to continually try to reach higher, go further, see over, and grasp something greater than you now know. Nobody knows who you are except God who has blessed you with potential. Everything created by God is blessed with potential. The most important principle of life is that God is a God of potential and he created everything with potential.

Remember the parable of Jesus in Matthew 25:15;

...he gave to EVERYMAN according to his several ability.

What you need to fulfill your dream is already in you in form of potential. Your only task is to discover it and harness it to bring you into your land of fulfillment.

The ability is in you, but your understanding of its usage is the key to your fulfillment. There is no one who is not gifted by God one way or the other.

You have within you all the qualities and elements that are necessary to make you a success. Your major task is the development of that gift that God has already given you.

Please, understand that, you are not disadvantaged. You have been given all you need to become the success God made you to be. You only need to accept responsibility for the release of that potential that is in you.

Your success in life in the pursuit of your dream is not determined by the potential alone, but by what you do with that potential.

Again, in that parable of Jesus in Matthew 25:14-15 we read that one servant was given five talents, the other was given two while the third was given one. But if you read further, you will discover that the same statement of commendation was made in respect of the first and the second men who put their talents to use. In other words, it is not whether you have five or whether you have two that matters, it is whether you put what you have to use.

DISCOVERING YOUR POTENTIAL

Your potential is given to you by God. It is the gift of God in you. Also, we have established the fact that potential is a gift or talent, which has its source in God.

Since God is the source of potential, then you need to consult Him in order to know your gift and talent. When you pray to God and ask Him to reveal to you what He puts in you, you will receive the answer. This is true according the assurance we have in Matthew 7:7-8;

Ask, and it shall be given you; seek, and ye shall find; knock, and it shall be opened unto you:

For every one that asketh receiveth; and he that seeketh findeth; and to him that knocketh it shall be opened.

In other words, prayer is an avenue by which God reveals your potential to you.

Prayer is very important because it is our means of constantly granting God permission to interfere in the affairs of man on earth. God can do anything He wants to do, but since He has given us the freewill to operate on earth, He can release on the earth only what we allow. You need to pray daily until you begin to see those great things that God has deposited in you. God reveals your potentials to you through prayers.

Also, the wisdom of God through the Bible is another channel for the discovery of your potential. When you are given to the study of the book of wisdom - the Bible - you will discover what God has put in you which can change your world. You cannot separate the gift of God in you from His Word. When you receive the truth of the Word of God, what God had deposited in you is made manifest.

Another way you can discover your potential is by looking inward into your inner man. Your inner man is always craving for physical expression. The gift in you does not want to remain dormant. Your major task is to know what your inner man is saying. This come by intuition; that is, to know something without being told. You just know it by an inward witness.

Now that you have understood what potential is and how to discover yours, it is time for you to learn how to release it for the fulfillment of your dream.

RELEASING YOUR POTENTIAL

The question now is how do I release my potential to achieve my dream?

The answer is WORK, WORK and WORK.

It is through work that your potential is released, and if you do not release it, you cannot fulfill your dream. It takes diligence, which is hard work in the right direction to release your potential. That potential can die with you if you do not release it.

You have a responsibility for the release of your potential to achieve your dream.

It takes work to achieve greatness. No one talks about greatness without work.

Work is not the same as a job. It is not a job that releases potential, it is work. Job only provides you a pay cheque at the end of the month.

Job according to Farrah Gray means; *"Just over Broke' that is, one pay cheque away from being evicted."*

Work is God's way of revealing your talents, abilities and capabilities. When you have a dream, then it is time to work out its fulfillment and that requires the use of your potential, but that potential is released by hard work. Work arises from the desire to contribute to the world's wealth and well-being by giving of what you have been given by God in form of potential.

It is only through work that you can do and become all that God originally intended for your life. God does not give potential for fun; He expects it to be released as you work it out through committed, smart and creative work. Potential without work remains untapped. It remains unused and untested. Another way to define work is the use of your God given abilities and faculties to do or perform a task.

Your purpose in life is a task, but you have been given potential to achieve it. It is as you commit yourself to work that the potential is released to accomplish the task. Do not go to the grave yard with that dream of yours, it has great possibilities but you must work out your potential to fulfill it.

Until you start working out your potential, you do not stand to benefit the world with the power that you are endowed with. You are created to work. Your refusal to work is not revealing the image of God that you are. If you don't work that potential, it remains dormant and useless. And God will not be happy about it.

Janice Krouskop once said; **"Without ambition one starts nothing, and without hard work one finishes nothing. Therefore, those who stretch their backbone to reach their wish bone will make things happen."**

It is only in the dictionary that you will see that success comes before work. But in real life, it is work before success. Work must come first before success can be achieved. Successful accomplishment of a dream is a direct product of hard work.

William Pedrin wrote this poem to corroborate the truth about work before success:

"No pain, no palm,

No cross, no crown,

No thorn, no throne,

No gall, no glory!"

Work is a must in order to release your potential. You cannot really know how much you can achieve until you put your hands to work. You are capable of doing more than you have done, but that can only be known through your commitment to work.

That gift in you is called potential, that talent in you is called potential. That divine endowment is called potential. But it is given to you for your accomplishment and it is your personal responsibility to understand, discover and release it. As you do so, you cannot but achieve the object of your dream.

The best preparation for good work tomorrow is to do good work today, because the good work of today is to discover your potential and release it to fulfill your dream so that tomorrow, you will generate great impact in your own generation.

Chapter 6: DOCUMENT YOUR DREAM

Take the time to write down carefully what you want to accomplish with your life. Writing down your goal makes you more decisive.

MIKE MURDROCK

When you write something down, it takes a life of its own. Suddenly, it becomes clear in your mind exactly what you want. Your dreams become clear to other people, because they can read what you plan to accomplish.

CONWAY STONE

Dream in a pragmatic way

ALDOUS HUXLEY

The dream you do not document in detail, its object you may not achieve. And, no matter how sharp you think your memory is, you cannot fulfill a dream that you did not write down in some details, because; the shortest pencil is sharper than the sharpest brain.

The act of documenting your dream in details has power to change your life. Until you are able to document your dream in detail by using sentences, graphs, charts, pictures etc. you cannot fully realize the object of that dream.

There is an enormous power in writing down what you want to do before you begin. That is why you must take the time to do series of writings, drawings and plotting your dream in a very clear term.

I want to admonish that, before you begin to pursue that dream in your heart, sit down and document it. Write it down, because, it will help you a lot in your bid to accomplish it.

God is the first writer. He values writing and believes so much in it according to Deuteronomy 10:1-4;

At that time the LORD said to me, "Chisel out two stone tablets like the first ones and come up to me on the mountain. Also make a wooden chest. I WILL WRITE ON THE TABLETS THE WORDS THAT WERE ON THE FIRST TABLETS, which you broke. Then you are to put them in the chest."

So I made the ark out of acacia wood and chiseled out two stone tablets like the first ones, and I went up on the mountain with the two tablets in my hands. THE LORD WROTE ON THESE TABLETS WHAT HE HAD WRITTEN BEFORE, the Ten Commandments he had proclaimed to you on the mountain, out of the fire, on the day of the assembly. And the LORD gave them to me. (NIV)

God told Moses that He would re-write what He wrote before, which Moses destroyed. That means God attaches much importance to documenting of issues in our lives. If that is not so, why did He re-write the ten commandment for Moses?

That Tablet contained God's instruction for His people to operate with as they followed the dream of getting to Canaan land.

The importance that God attached to writing is also revealed in Jeremiah 30:2;

Thus speaketh the LORD God of Israel, saying, WRITE THEE ALL THE WORDS THAT I HAVE SPOKEN UNTO THEE IN A BOOK.

God actually commanded Jeremiah to write in a book. In the same manner, you must write what you see in your mind as your dream in a book if you want to achieve it.

Also, in the classic book of vision, Habakkuk 2:1-2, it was noted;

I will stand upon my watch, and set me upon the tower, and will watch to see what he will say unto me, and what I shall answer when I am reproved.

And the LORD answered me, and said, **WRITE THE VISION, AND MAKE IT PLAIN UPON TABLES, THAT HE MAY RUN THAT READETH IT.**

We are commanded by God to WRITE THE VISION.

In other words document the dream, make it plain upon the table. That means write it in details in your dream book, so that he may run that reads it. That simply means so that you may know how to pursue that dream to fulfillment.

There is power in writing your dream in a book. It really helps you to follow it through to fulfillment.

In the last chapter of the Bible, the book of Revelation chapter 1:11;

...WHAT THOU SEEST, WRITE IN A BOOK, and send it unto the seven churches which are in Asia; unto Ephesus, and unto Smyrna, and unto Pergamos, and unto Thyatira, and unto Sardis, and unto Philadelphia, and unto Laodicea.

God sent an angel to instruct John to write the vision he had seen. Why was it so important for him to write the vision? This is because documenting of issues is so important to God for the fulfillment of His purpose for man.

And at the end of each letter to the churches, he said; ***"he that has ears let him hear what the Spirit says to the church"***.

That simply means that, the dream you receive is what the Spirit of God is saying to you and then you have to write it down so as to follow it through to fulfillment.

I believe that from all the scriptural references above, it is so clear that God is a committed writer.

And since we are created in His image, we must be committed to writing down our dreams and vision.

Two studies conducted by Massachusetts Mutual and AT & T concluded that businesses that have written business plan succeed. According to both studies, only 40% of businesses have written business plan that they follow. And those businesses are the ones that succeed (David Gunpter Communications).

Paul J. Meyer of Success Motivation Institute once said; *"I would like to repeat the critical importance of committing your plan to writing. It cannot be overemphasized!"*

The way to begin in the exercise of documenting of dream is to do the following:

Develop a Dream Book

Go and buy a notebook or a file containing plain papers that can be attached to that file where you can write your dream. This step is very crucial for your fulfillment. Write on the cover page very boldly **"MY DREAM/VISION IN LIFE"**

This notebook becomes the place where you document all your dreams in life. This notebook should be kept separate from other books where you write other things. It must contain only your dream and any other thing related to the fulfillment of that dream.

Now I want us to be practical in this stage. In case you already have a notebook at home or a file with plain paper in your office for this exercise, I will tell you the next thing to do. But in case you do not have one yet, I advise that you close this book now, get to the nearest store around you where you can get a notebook and a pen to do this serious business. When that is done, the next step is to:

Write your Mission Statement

I have described Mission Statement in detail in the previous chapter. Your Mission Statement must be in direct relation to your dream in life. Try to reduce all your dreams into one statement called Mission Statement. That statement describes your dream as your person. It shows the world who you are and what you want to do. Your mission is the pointer to what you want to do in life. It is one statement describing what you want to achieve in life. A Mission Statement can give you a general purpose for all your activities.

Farrah Gray concludes this point by saying; **"Perfect your elevator pitch'. You've got to** *be able to articulate your point in one sentence or you'll never get anywhere in business."*

You know that your life is a business and you must approach it so. You must be able to describe your dream in one sentence, and that is your Mission Statement.

Write Down Your Dreams In Details And Be Specific

Your ability to think through all the possibilities about your dream matters a lot. Do not just write it down but also be specific about the dream. Be exact and detailed.

It is not enough to write down what you want to do; you must be able to write it down in such a way that it will be detailed enough for you to know what you must do to achieve it. Since you already have a Mission Statement, all the things you want to do towards the accomplishment of that Mission Statement is the detailed version of your dream.

For instance, you have a dream of becoming a multimillionaire. That is a great dream. But you must go ahead to think of what business you will do to attain the multimillion; who your customers will be, what product will be, where your product will sell, what kind of training you need in order to acquired the necessary skills for the business, what you want to do with the millions when it begins to come in. All these are the details of the dream of becoming a multimillionaire.

Please understand that it is not enough to have a dream, you must write down the details of your dream in your dream book.

Now I want you to look at your dream/vision book and read out your Mission Statement.

Then what must be your dream to accomplish this Mission Statement. Begin to think now and then; begin to write down the details of your dream.

This exercise can take days, weeks or even months because you may not be able to get the details on the spot. But the truth is that you must begin now. Do not just write what you know how to do, you may not know how to do it now, but later you will learn how to do it. It may look impossible, but in as much as it will lead to the achievement of your Mission Statement, just go ahead and write it down.

No matter how big it is for you now and even if nobody in this world has done it before, just go ahead and write it down in details using all your creative thinking faculties as you keep looking at it, what to do to achieve it will come to you sooner than you know.

It was Henry Ford, who said; *"One of the greatest discoveries a man makes; one of his greatest surprises is to find he can do what he was afraid he couldn't do."*

That is the truth; you can do that thing no matter how impossible it may appear now. And by the time you do it, you will find out that *"It is kind of fun to do the impossible"* as Walt Disney puts it.

The impossible can be done. All you need is to write it down in form of a dream first. And as you look at it, then the 'how to' accomplish it will be revealed to you because the mind attracts what it dwells on repeatedly.

As you write down the details of your dream, what you have or what you do not have notwithstanding; you will accomplish it in no time. All you need is to stay on and hold fast to your dream.

Chapter 7: DEVELOP A PLAN

The majority of people meet with failure because they lack the persistence to create new plans to take the place of failed plans.

MARK VICTOR HANSEN

Success does not require a super intellect. It does require a dream with PLANS to reach a goal.

KEN GAUB

"You want to set a goal that is big enough that in the process of achieving it you become someone worth becoming.

JIM ROHN

Planning is a major key to accomplishment of any given task in life. Only those who develop a plan can fulfill the objects of their dream. A plan is the roadmap to your destination. Your destination is the fulfillment of your dream, but the map to get you there is the plan you have to develop.

Also, a plan is the architectural design for the house you are to build. Your dream is likened to a building, but there has to be a clear design in place to follow in putting up the building. Your dream is your destiny placed in front of your, but your plan is the step by step roadmap that you will follow to take you to that destiny.

The Amplified version of Proverbs 24:3 says;

***ANY ENTERPRISE IS BUILT BY WISE PLANNING,** becomes strong through common sense, and profits wonderfully by keeping abreast of the facts.*

Your dream is likened to building an enterprise and planning is required to do that. Nothing can substitute for planning in our bid to fulfill a dream. There is no man who can successfully accomplish any dream without a well designed plan. I believe that, no one plans to fail, but people fail to plan. And failure to plan automatically results in failure to accomplish a dream. That means one of the causes of failure in life is failure to plan.

Planning is what helps in the translation of your desire into action. That is why quality time must be invested into the planning process. It is not what you rush to do, because your plan must be detailed enough to accommodate every aspect of all the issues relating to your dream.

Lester R. Bittel, the author of The Nine Master Keys of Management said; *"Good plans shape good decisions. That's why good planning helps to make elusive dreams come true."*

No one has ever built a house without a building plan. No successful business or empire is ever built in life without a blueprint. The blueprint is the plan. In your plan, the details of how you will relate with people, how you will acquire the relevant skills, how you will acquire the material and financial resources and how you are going to utilize and coordinate them for the fulfillment of your dream must be put into consideration.

However, planning is of different types, but I will focus on one that is very important in relation to fulfillment of dream, which is Strategic Planning.

Kenneth R. Andrew of Harvard Business School defines strategic planning as **"Corporate Strategy; the pattern of decision in a company that determines and reveals its objectives, purpose or goals and produces the principal policies and plans for achieving these goals and defines the range of business the company is to pursue, the kind of economic and human organization it is or intends to be and the nature of the economic and non-economic contributions** *it intends to make to its shareholders, employees customers and communities."*

This definition of strategic planning is very detailed in the sense that it talks about all the elements to be put into consideration in planning. It involves a long term objectives to be accomplished and the methods to achieve them.

Strategic planning the process by which leaders of an organization determine what it intends to be in the future and how it will get there. To put it another way, they develop a vision for the organization's future and determine the necessary priorities, procedures, and operations (strategies) to achieve that vision. Included are measurable goals which are realistic and attainable, but also challenging; emphasis is on long-term goals and strategies, rather than short-term (such as annual) objectives. Strategic planning assumes that certain aspects of the future can be created or influenced by the organization.

Strategic planning is ongoing; and according to Pfeiffer et al. in their book Understanding Applied Strategic Planning: A Manager's Guide, it is the process of self-examination, the confrontation of difficult choices, and the establishment of priorities.

The more enlightened you are in strategically planning your dream, the faster your accomplishment and the stronger and long lasting your building (dream). The truth of the matter is that God will not plan for you. Planning is a personal responsibility.

Also, strategic planning is about being futuristic in your planning process. It involves forecasting into the future to capture your expectation and then setting a plan for the realization of the object of your forecast. Forecasting simply means to predict, to estimate before hand. And that is what strategic planning is all about.

It is interesting to know that the big corporations of the world such as those listed in Fortune 500 published by Fortune Magazine engage strictly in art of strategic planning. And that is why their successes know no bound.

Few years ago, I was at a beach in Badagry, Nigeria with the youth of my church and the man of God, my mentor Dr David Oyedepo came to address us. What baffled me most was that the only thing he told us to do was to engage in strategic planning for the fulfillment of our purposes in life.

In his address on that day, he said; "Spend time in strategic planning for actualizing your purpose. God plans for no man, every man that desires fulfillment of his purpose will have to engage in strategic planning to make it a reality."

Then I thought; 'This man is a pastor, why is he talking about strategic planning?' I had always thought that pastors do not need to plan; they needed to just pray and things would happen but I was wrong. Then I discovered that his success in ministry is a result of his commitment to strategic planning. That is why he became a world renowned pastor of a church with the largest auditorium on earth; Faith Tabernacle, situated in Canaan land, Ota, Nigeria.

That encounter changed my life as daily I began to engage in strategic planning and not just having a plan. Now I have five years, ten years, twenty, forty years et cetera. plans for my life, well documented in my dream book. This book in your hand is part of the outcome of my strategic planning. Planning helps in having a sound direction of how to go about the fulfillment of our dreams in life.

Donald Goss once said; **"Direction is simply the exercise of planning how you are going to get from Point A to Point B and then focusing on it."**

You need to engage in strategic planning too in order to accomplish your dream in life. But you must understand that strategic planning is for the purpose of fulfilling your dream or vision in life and you must act on it, as John Naisbitt said; **"Strategic Planning is worthless unless there is first a strategic vision."**

Goal Setting

A goal is a dream with a date on it, because, a goal is nothing more than a dream with a time limit.

I want you to know that goal is not the same as plan. But you cannot have a plan without setting goals. As a matter of fact, the essence of planning is to reach a goal. The major challenge of not having a goal is that, you can spend your life running up and down the field and never score. The main aim and objective of every football team in any match is not to play well; their chief aim is to score as many goals as they can. That is why there are goal posts on every football field. All the running and dribbling with the ball on the field of play is aimed at scoring a goal. That is why when any player scores a goal, all team members including their fans will begin to run, jump, clap and celebrate. This is because the aim has been accomplished. A goal has been scored.

You cannot celebrate your dream until you have been able to achieve your goal. That is why you need to take time to set goals for your desired accomplishment. When you have set your goals, you will know for sure where your efforts will be directed. That is why successful people succeed. They are goal setters and goal getters.

Arnold Glasow once said; ***"In life, as in football, you won't go far unless you know where the goal posts are."***

Goal setting is very essential to the fulfillment of your dream; you must commit to it.

What is a Goal?

A goal can be defined as the end result of ultimate accomplishment toward which an effort is directed. A goal is the mark desired to hit; the sign post to ones end; a state of affairs that a man intended to achieve and which terminates when achieved.

A goal is a personal Mission Statement; it is a point marking the finish of a race; it is the object of one's effort, it is a target. To set goals means to define a course of action without distraction; to burn the bridge; to bring oneself under an oath; to declare one's fixed and unalterable decision.

Now that you have a dream well and clearly written down; you have written your Mission Statement and the details of your strategic plans are on paper; my question is; what are your goals? This is very crucial to your fulfillment in life. It is goal setting that gives you focus and clarity of what you want. Goal setting helps your passion to grow, it eliminates tension, gives you divine speed, and it helps you have a balanced life because you will always know the exact things to do and where to go per time. David J. Schwarz in his book **"The Magic of Thinking Big" said; "Nothing happens; no forward steps are taken until a goal is established."**

Elements of Goals

All goals are expected to have the following elements;

Uniqueness: - Your goal must be unique because your dream is not the same as other people's dreams and you are the one who set your goal. That makes it unique.

Inspirational: - Inspiration means to be inspired. Your goal is based on your inspired thought that is; the dream of your heart. That goal must inspire you to move towards your dream. Andrew Carnegie once said; *"If you want to be happy, set a goal that commands your thoughts, liberates your energy, and inspires your hopes."*

Specificity: - Goals are specific things you want to accomplish. It must not be a vague mind description of your desire, but a specific object of your desire.

Documentation: - Your goal must be clearly written down so that you will always know what to do.

Realizability: - Your goal must be a realizable one. You know what you can achieve, so be realistic based on the facts available to you.

Harmonimity: - Your goal should be in harmony with your core values & beliefs. It must align with your dream.

Timeliness: - Your goal must be with date. There must be a time limit on your goal. That means there is a time to begin and a time to end and once it ends, it is accomplished.

It is time for you to begin to set your own goal in harmony with your dream. You have to eliminate all those things that are not healthy for the fulfillment of your dream. Some desires or likes have to be murdered if they are not in line with your dream.

That is why goals must be unique since what Mr. A wants to achieve is not always the same as what Mr. B wants to achieve.

Daily Agenda

This is part of the planning and goal settings process.

Your daily agenda is the list of what you want to accomplish within the next 24 hours. Your daily agenda must be in harmony with your dream and goal.

Dr Mike Murdock once said; **"What you do daily determines what you become permanently. I cannot change you until am able to change what you do daily."**

Your understanding of this truth will unlock your future and eliminates what is not healthy for your fulfillment. Also, you need to set your priorities in your daily agenda. You must be able to list your daily agenda items in order of importance based on your personal assessment. You must know the first thing to do and then the second, third and so on, on a daily basis. When your priorities become habitual, you will unlock your potentials. When you focus on your priorities, you will be able to eliminate all forms of distraction that can bring confusion as you follow your dream. You must focus on the tasks that you know are worthy of all your attention and time.

However, do all you can not to over schedule your daily agenda; you should know your capacity per day. You cannot finish every thing in one day. That is why you must take the time to write down only what you know you can complete in a day so that you will not be discouraged when you are unable to complete the list on your daily agenda.

Your daily activities determine your weekly results which determine your monthly outcomes and that ultimately determine your yearly outputs.

It was Joseph Ross who said; **"It takes time to succeed because success is merely a natural reward of taking time to do anything well."**

You need to develop a plan; engage in strategic planning by forecasting, set goals with time limit.

Also, develop a daily agenda; a list of what you must do daily in line with your dream and goals. You need to task yourself to be committed to the agenda. That is how you can fulfill your dream.

Friend, it is time for you to predetermine the objectives you want to accomplish. Think big, act big and set out to accomplish big results in life as you follow your dream.

It may be that those who do most, dream most.

STEPHEN LEACOCK

Chapter 8: DECISIONS: THE KEY FACTORS

The difference between the high achiever and low achiever is this: The high achiever almost always makes decisions before he's ready to move.

ROBERT SCHULLER

You will never leave where you are until you decide where you would rather be.

MIKE MURDOCK

Success will not happen unless you choose to make it happen. Success is not a lucky break. It is not a divine right. It is not an accident of birth. Success is a choice.

RICK PITINO

There is great power in decision making. No matter how big, great and positive your dream, no matter how well defined your plans, and no matter how original, inspirational, realistic and timely your goals, until you make certain decisions on your way to your dream of success, you may never get there. You have to decide on what to focus on. You have to decide on what you will spend your time on. You have to decide where you will go and where you will not go. Your decision has the power to push you into those things that are needed to be done in order to fulfill your dream.

No one will do the deciding for you because no one does the dreaming, the planning and the setting of goals for you. It is a personal responsibility which you must accept because, in any activity in life, the first step to success is decision making. And it is either you will decide for your life, or life will decide for you.

However, in this chapter, I want to take time to examine certain areas of decision that you must make in order to effectively fulfill your dream. It is in your moments of decision that your destiny is shaped. That is why it is your responsibility to decide where you are going and what you want for your life, then and only then will you begin to see the signposts that point the way. Your decision has the power to unlock your future, therefore;

Decide to Learn

Dr David Oyedepo once said; *"**No matter how gifted you are, it is how studious you are*** *that determines how colourful you will become mentally."*

Learning is a must if you must grow and the day you stop learning is the day you stopped growing. And you must keep growing if you must fulfill your dream.

Learning is an activity of the mind because the mind has the ability to acquire and store information which can be used when required. That is why it is important not to stop learning, because, the day a man stops learning, is the day he starts dying, no matter his age. That is the reality of life. No one has ever succeeded in life without taking time to learn all about his pursuit. As a matter of fact, the more learned you are in your field the more command you gain and ultimately, the more respect you earn.

However, it is so demoralizing to see people running from place to place trying to get a dream fulfill and yet they have never taken the time to learn what they need to know about that dream.

There are people who have written books relating to their dream and they have shared the stories of how they have been able to fulfill their dreams. You need to get their materials and study them to help you learn what to do in your own pursuit in life.

There is no self made man, all men are made by what they know and how can you know without learning. Learning is the way to avoid shame and to secure divine approval. It is through learning that you can fulfill your destiny.

In the Gospel of Matthew 9:13, Jesus said;

But GO YE AND LEARN what that meaneth, I will have mercy, and not sacrifice: for I am not come to call the righteous, but sinners to repentance.

Also the great Apostle Paul, in his letter to his son in ministry, Timothy said in first Timothy 4:13;

Till I come, give attendance to reading, to exhortation, to doctrine.

Learning must be given attention and it must be a continuous exercise if you must continue to grow. Life is designed for continuous growth.

Learning delivers great benefits to us among which are:

Knowledge

One of the end results of learning is knowledge. Knowledge is acquired through the process of learning. Knowledge is defined as the sum or range of what has been perceived, discovered or learned. It also means familiarity, awareness gained through the art of study or through experience.

Every man of exploit is a man of knowledge and knowledge is the gateway to freedom and liberty.

In John 8:32, Jesus said;

And ye shall know the truth, and the truth shall make you free.

Also King Solomon in the book of Proverbs 11:9 said;

An hypocrite with his mouth destroyeth his neighbour: but THROUGH KNOWLEDGE SHALL THE JUST BE DELIVERED.

That means your success in life is directly linked to your knowledge in life. And your liberty from stagnation and lack of fulfillment answers to your knowledge base. What you know cannot be separated from what you will accomplish in the race of life. That is why you need to crave after knowledge. You need to decide to learn as you go on in life so as to overcome destruction, unfulfillment and failure, as the book of wisdom says in Hosea 4:6;

My people are destroyed for lack of knowledge: because thou hast rejected knowledge, I will also reject thee, that thou shalt be no priest to me: seeing thou hast forgotten the law of thy God, I will also forget thy children

The only way to avoid failure is to keep acquiring knowledge by continuous learning.

And the most powerful channel of acquiring knowledge is by reading. Readers are winners. You must give attention to reading in order to remove the stress in your way of accomplishment. However, you must apply what you know as Bruce Lee puts it

"Knowing is not enough; we must apply; willing is not enough; we must do."

Understanding

This is the way of life. Learning leads to understanding. To understand means to gain insight into the depth of an issue. It means to come to know or become aware of something. To understand means to grasp the meaning of something, by learning or studying.

When your understanding comes alive, your dream will be accomplished without stress.

I love the story of Daniel in the Bible. God gave Daniel great wisdom and ability to see visions and that made him a great man in the land of Babylon. He was so gifted that he was able to provide answers to issues that even the wise men of the king could not provide answers to. By virtue of this, Daniel was highly exalted above all men in the land of Babylon.

Daniel made a startling statement in Daniel 9:2;

In the first year of his reign I DANIEL UNDERSTOOD BY BOOKS the number of the years, whereof the word of the LORD came to Jeremiah the prophet, that he would accomplish seventy years in the desolations of Jerusalem.

---

is reign I DANIEL UNDERSTOOD BY BOOKS the number of the years, whereof the word of the LORD came to Jeremiah the prophet, that he would accomplish seventy years in the desolations of Jerusalem.

Despite the gift of God in Daniel's life, he was still committed to learning by reading books.

Understanding is the way of life as David said in Psalms 119:144;

The righteousness of thy testimonies is everlasting: give me understanding, and I shall live.

You have to be committed to the art of learning about the issues of life as it relates to your dream until knowledge and understanding dawn on you. And when that happens, you become a man of exploit who always knows what to do.

Creativeness

When you commit yourself to constant learning, your creative ability will improve; and it takes the use of your creative imagination to be able to turn your dream into reality. To be creative means to be able to create a new thing out of an existing or old thing; to be able to locate a new and a better way of doing what others have done before. It means to be able to make imaginative use of the limited resources available.

Creativity is the outcome of ideas gained through learning. And it is ideas that rule the world. You need to have a sound idea in order to have a sound working knowledge of what is required in accomplishing your tasks.

A creative mind is a mind stocked with creative ideas that can turn dream into reality with speed. Therefore when you decide to learn, you will gain knowledge, understanding and you will be exposed to creative ideas that will help you to turn your dream into reality.

It is the application of knowledge and understanding that put you in charge in your pursuit of excellence.

I want to conclude this segment by the words of the young *"realionaire"* Farray Gray; who said; **"I began studying the personality traits of highly successful people from all walks of life so I could emulate their successes in my own life. A public library card gave me access to study our country's greatest** *success stories. Reading about their trials, tribulations and triumph inspired me to stay on my course."*

Decide To Rejoice

Joy is a catalyst for success in every pursuit of life. It takes joy to gain access to mental excellence and you need to be mentally alert to fulfill your dream in life.

In fact, the more enthusiastic you are, the more inspired you become; and it takes inspiration to follow your dream.

No matter what situation you face in life, you have to make a decision to always be joyful. The ideas you need to pursue your dream will only flow in the atmosphere of joy; not in a place of sadness and depression. It takes excitement to gain access to mental excellence.

Nehemiah 8:10;

...neither be ye sorry, for the joy of the Lord is your strength.

You need energy and strength to fulfill your dream and that will answer to joy.

Thomas R. Dewar once said; **"Minds are like parachutes they only function when opened."**

It takes joy for your mind to be opened to great possibilities. Your mind will function well in the atmosphere of cheers, joy, and celebration with excitement. You must decide to be enthusiastic in your pursuit. This means to be excited about your dream. Every waking day should take you towards your fulfillment as you rejoice every morning for yet another opportunity of life.

In my years of study of the life of great men of exploits, I have found out this common denominator in their lives and that is excitement and enthusiasm. Despite the great challenges that many of them faced, they stayed balanced rejoicing in the midst of those challenges. It is a matter of decision. They have made the choice to celebrate no matter what happens. They chose to be on top of the situations, rather than allow situations to take control of them.

The state of your heart has a lot to do with the state of your life. If you don't decide to rejoice now, you may not see the full realization of your dream because lack of joy will limit your rate of motion as you go on.

The only way to overcome challenges in form of hardship is to rejoice. You must be able to laugh at your problems. Decide to be happy for the privilege God has given to you to be alive and have a dream. Always remember that life is a privilege. Joy and happiness are produced not so much by great pieces of good fortune that seldom happen as by little advantages that occur every day. Look at yourself in a mirror every morning and rejoice that you are made in the image of God, and that you have been given the gift of another day to follow your dream.

It was Sebastian Chamfort that said; **"The most wasted of all our days are those in which we have not laughed."**

Laughter must be your way of life in the pursuit of your dream and that has to be by a decision that you have carefully made.

The great Apostle Paul, who suffered so much in the hand of the Roman Soldiers, emphasized the place of joy in the fulfillment of destiny. He was in the prison and yet he wrote to the church admonishing them to rejoice.

Philippians 3:1;

Finally, my brethren, rejoice in the Lord. ...

Philippians 4:4;

Rejoice in the Lord alway: and again I say, Rejoice.

Apostle Paul gained access to such an amazing inspiration by virtue of his excited lifestyle. He was always rejoicing and celebrating in the midst of his predicament. No matter what is happening in your life now, your rejoicing is crucial to your success.

Decide to stop worrying and being anxious about issues. Life has its challenges and it is what you do in the midst of your challenges that determine the end result.

Your decision to rejoice is imperative to your success in life. You can be the designer of your life or the victim of your circumstances; it is up to you. That is why you have to make the choice not to allow life's issues to weigh you down. You must take charge of the circumstances of life as you rejoice at all times. That dream is realizable and accomplishable, just decide to rejoice and the way to go about it will be revealed to you in no time.

Decide To Association Wisely

Now you have documented your dream, you have developed the strategic plan and the goals you want to reach which will be the ultimate fulfillment of your dream. Also, you have decided to rejoice always as you pursue your dream. It is now time for you to make decision about who you have to associate with in the pursuit of your dream.

Of course you know that if you keep relating closely with those who have no dreams, goals or those whose dreams and goals are totally different from yours, you will not be able to fulfill your dream. The people you move with and the company you keep have a lot to do with the fulfillment of your dream.

To fulfill your dream, you must associate with people of faith who know how to get result. You must associate with people who have won; those who are climbing up. You must talk to people smarter than you; listen to those more spiritual than you; ask questions from those who are more successful than you.

Your association determines your destination. Many people don ot really understand the importance of this truth.

Let me illustrate with this analogy; if you have a ticket to fly to America, you are not going to board the same plane with your friend who is going to

Saudi Arabia. These are two different routes. And if each one must get to his destination; each one has to board his own plane. No matter how close your friendship is, since you do not have the same dream, your route to your dreams will be different.

Wisdom demands that you look for those who are going where you are going, those who have the kind of result you are looking for; those who can help you to get to the fulfillment of your dream. This is one of the major decisions you need to make at the early stage of the pursuit of your dream. If you do not make that decision now, before you begin, it may draw you back in the pursuit of your dream.

Decide now. There are people that God has designed to help you in life; Look out for them and associate with them. There are always people who will help you. Just keep looking until you find them. Do not give up, keep asking for help. That's not begging, that's investing in your future. There are a lot of good people in the world. Do not ever let anyone tell you differently.

No matter what your dream is, it is your association that determines your destination. Do not ever go with someone who is not pursuing the same dream as yours. If you do, you can easily be distracted and that will amount to the abortion of your dream. You can learn from him, but do not go with him since he is not going to where you are going.

Proverbs 13:20;

He that walketh with wise men shall be wise: but a companion of fools shall be destroyed.

My life is a very good example. I have associated with Dr. David Oyedepo since 1997 and today I am an ordained Pastor and author of books. The grace upon him has rubbed-off on me as I keep walking with him since that time.

Also, the books and tapes of great leaders like Kenneth E. Hagin, Dr. Myles Munroe, Dr. Creflo Dollar, Joyce Meyer, Dag Heward Mill, Ben Carson, Anthony Robins, John C. Maxwell, Mensa Otabil, Sam Adeyemi, to mention but a few, have become my greatest companions over the years. My success today is not far fetched from the kind of companies and associations I have kept over the years.

Who you go with determines where you arrive at. Decide to go with those who are going to where you are going and there will be safe arrival at your destination.

I like the way Charles Jones puts it; ***"You'll remain the same way you are today in five years, except for two things: the books you read and the people with whom you walk."***

That is an amazing reality of life. Friendship is by choice. You can make a choice of who to associate with because it will determine the events in your life. If you associate with lazy and negative people, you become lazy and negative. Change your association today, if you know that it will not take you to your dream land.

Decide To Serve

Service is the pathway to greatness in life. Until you are ready to serve, you are not prepared to shine. It takes stewardship to mount the throne of leadership. Accomplishment in life is a direct product of stewardship.

This is one of the greatest decisions you must make as you pursue your dream. Your dream is a seed from God and that seed was given to you for the purpose of improving the lot of other people. The fulfillment of your dream must bring happiness, joy, comfort and fulfillment to people.

If you are a people thinker, you are a great leader. But if you are only thinking of yourself, you may end up is slavery.

Your dream in life should be a solution to the problems of the people around the world. Any dream that is self centered will end up as a doom.

Any dream that is not after the well being of mankind is not of God and if God is left out of the picture of your life, you are bound to fail. Our best, no matter how good is incomplete if we leave God out of the picture.

If you check through the biographies of men of exploits since the world began, you will find this common factor of service in their lives.

Your decision to serve others is what brings you into the realm of speedy accomplishment of your own dream.

- ✓ During one of my recent studies on this subject of service, I come up with the following thoughts:

- ✓ Service is your ticket into the realm of glorification.

- ✓ If you refuse to serve others, you will be starved by others.

- ✓ Stardom is a direct product of service.

- ✓ Your shining in life is achieved by your service in life.

- ✓ To escape stinking is to embrace service.

- ✓ Sincere service ensures a secured future.

- ✓ The security of your destiny is a product of the sincerity of your service to mankind.

- ✓ Leadership begins with giving others the first place before yourself.

- ✓ The level of your greatness in life is a function of the level of your service to mankind.

You have no excuse for not getting involved in serving people. Service makes room for you to release your potential to the world.

The truth is that, I did not know I could write or author any book. But when I gave myself over to the study of the purpose of God for my life and God began to reveal to me how great He has endowed man with great potentials. Because countless millions of people are ignorant of these hidden treasures in them, it became a concern to me and a burden was placed in me to let people know how powerful they are when they discover what heaven has put in them. That was the passion that brought me into writing of books so as to share with people the purpose and plan of God for creating them. I did not know that I could be as productive as this until I began to put my gift to work in service of humanity. Also, it was in the process of my kingdom service that I discovered my destiny as a Pastor, called by God to serve my generation.

God's perspective of success is reaching beyond ourselves and helping others in specific ways. Great men think others, small men think self. If you must become great in life let your dream have an end result of service to humanity. If you cannot serve others, you cannot out shine others.

In the Words of Jesus to his disciples in Mark 10:43-45; He said;

But so shall it not be among you: but WHOSOEVER WILL BE GREAT AMONG YOU, SHALL BE YOUR MINISTER:

AND WHOSOEVER OF YOU WILL BE THE CHIEFEST, SHALL BE SERVANT OF ALL.

For even the Son of man came not to be ministered unto, but to minister, and to give his life a ransom for many.

In other words, if you are seeking position of greatness, you must seek to serve others. It is your service to others that will usher you into that position of greatness. It does not come by chance or by accident.

Charles Spurgeon once said; *"Feel for others... in your wallet"* and Eleanor Roosevelt puts it this way; *"When you cease to make a contribution, you begin to die."*

Abundant living is a product of three major factors which include; how you care for others, how you dare for others and how you share with others.

Friend, your decisions to learn, rejoice, associate wisely and serve others are most crucial to ultimate accomplishment of your dream in life. You have to make up your mind and make the right choices on your way to fulfillment, because, there is a loftier ambition than merely to stand high in the world. It is to stoop down and lift mankind a little higher.

> ***Be willing to be uncomfortable. Be comfortable being uncomfortable. It may get tough, but it's a small price to pay for living a dream.***
>
> **PETER MCWILLIAMS**

Chapter 9: DARE YOUR DREAM

None of the Secret of Success will work unless you do; often, the simple answer to your problem is 'GO TO WORK'

JOHN MASON

'I can't do it' never yet accomplished anything; 'I will try' has performed wonders.

GEORGE P. BURNHAM

Do not let your learning lead to knowledge; let your learning lead to action.

JIM ROHN

Perhaps the most valuable result of all education is the ability to make yourself do things you have to do, when it ought to be done whether you like it or not.

THOMAS HUXLEY

No man can fulfill any dream or vision without practical commitment to the tasks involved. However, for every dream to be fulfilled, the dreamer must dare the dream. He is obligated to do the task involved in carrying out the dream. It is your decision to dare your dream that determines its ultimate accomplishment. It takes practical commitment on the part of the dreamer to his dream to have the dream fulfilled.

In my many years of study about successful men, I have found out that the men who fulfill their dreams are those who actually put dream into action. It is the practical pursuit of the dream that leads to its fulfillment. It is action that actually turns any dream into reality as Marlon Smith, the youth motivational trainer puts it when he said; **"A Vision without action is a wish, and wishes have no substance."**

And as you know by now that responsibility is the price for greatness. You must accept responsibility for the fulfillment of your dream.

Now that you have written your dreams in details, you have clearly designed your plan; you have made your decisions to pursue your dream. All those steps are essential and without them, you cannot fulfill your dream. The most interesting part of the issue is that those steps itemized above can become useless if the correct actions are not taken at the correct time.

How do you think it is possible for a man, who has a dream of traveling from Nigeria to London realize his dream without taking the practical steps of obtaining an International Passport, applying for a Visa and obtaining his flight ticket?

That dream becomes a balloon dream because it lacks the necessary actions.

Action is the leg you put into your vision/dream. Without a leg, no man can walk, without action, plans remain useless and dreams become a mirage. You can have lights, you can have camera, but nothing happens until you take action. The truth is that nothing happens until you take the necessary action irrespective of your plans and goals. Success does not answer to dream, plans and goals as much as it does to the practical actions taken towards the dream.

Habakkuk 2:2;

...Write the vision, and make it plain upon tables, THAT HE MAY RUN that readeth it.

What this means is that the essence of writing down your dream and setting your goals is to run as you read it. To run in this context means to take corresponding action on your dream. No matter how sound and great your dreams, plans and goals are, until you take action the reality is not in view. Nothing can take the place of active work in your bid to fulfill a dream. Work is a must and work is the action which is the responsibility you must accept.

Although you cannot do everything at a time, nevertheless you must begin from where you are, by taking that small action now. It is the combination of small actions on a daily basis that lead to the fulfillment of your dream. No matter how small an action is, if you do not take it you will not get to the fulfillment of your dream.

In real life, lots of people know what to do, but few people actually do what they know. Knowing is not enough! You must take action and great things are achievable by taking series of little steps. The little step you take today prepares you for the greater steps tomorrow, which will lead to your ultimate fulfillment.

Martin Luther King Jr. said; ***"If you cannot fly, run; if you cannot run, walk; if you cannot walk, crawl. By all means, keep moving."***

You must keep taking action daily towards your dream if you want it to become a reality. There is no way you would have the fruit without first climbing the tree. But the most challenging issue with people is that they want the fruit, yet are afraid of climbing the tree. No one will do it for you. You must accept responsibility for your life, because, well done is better than well said. No matter what you keep saying, what you do is the key to your fulfillment. People are tired of hearing about your dream; they want to see it practically fulfilled. There is no way you can win in a game that you did not play. You have to work to be fulfilled. And you do not really know how great you can accomplish until you put your hand to work. Your work is the action you take to fulfill your dream.

My question is what is your dream in life? What plans have you put in place? Have you set your goals? Then, what is your daily agenda? In your daily agenda, have you set your priorities based on your dream?

If you cannot answer these simple questions in details, then you are not fully ready to fulfill your dream.

Dreams are worthless if you only dream and do not take any action to reach the goals you have set. By now, when someone asks you, 'What do you want in life?' You should be able to answer by reading out your Mission Statement, details of your dream, your plans and goals. Your daily actions must directly relate to your dream. What you are doing daily determines how you will fulfill your destiny. Be careful of negative actions. A negative action is when you are doing things that have no correlation with your dream. It is moving in a wrong direction.

For instance, having written down my Mission Statement; I took practical action to write and to read from time to time materials that are related to my discovered purpose and the books I am writing. This gives me inspiration from those who are ahead of me in my line business and I am able to make reference to them, and then share their thoughts with others who read my books. I believe you have a reflection of this in this book in your hand. That is my action daily, and as I do that, I began to do it better and better until it has become part of me. I am never satisfied in a day when I have not read and written my thoughts in my study note. That is the power of action.

Also, as a preacher, teacher and a leadership coach, I look out for opportunities daily in order to prepare me for my speaking and teaching assignment. What I am doing is putting leg into my dream by practical commitment.

It does not matter what your dreams are, you have to wake up to do it. It is your responsibility to dream and execute your dreams as you drive yourself to the finishing lines of your purpose for living.

Take Action In Prayer

One of the major steps you must take is prayer. Prayer is a must if you want to achieve your dream and reach your goal. Your daily prayer life is very crucial to the successful accomplishment of your dream. Your dream is inseparable from God's purpose for your life and that dream is an inspiration from God. That is why you have to commit it to God to give you direction on how to fulfill it.

You need to take that documented dream, plans and goals to God in prayer daily. No matter what we know as human, God is still supreme and He already knows the end of every man before his beginning. Though you may not always get what you want, as long as you can pray about your dream, you cannot fail to have it accomplished.

Dreams often flounder when we neglect to make God our partner and ask His advice. We need to learn that we must to rely on God constantly for His help.

Proverbs 16:3;

Commit thy works unto the LORD, and thy thoughts shall be established.

When you form the habit of committing your dreams unto God, He will always help you to fulfill it because He is the inspiration behind your dream.

Dr Mike Murdock once said; **"One hour with God could easily reveal to you the fatal** *flaws in your most carefully laid plans. He who succeeds in prayer succeeds."*

The way you communicate with God in terms of asking for His help in the pursuit of your dream is a proof of your readiness to fulfill that dream. If you do not ask God for help, you cannot go far in the race of life.

In my years of research about the secrets of men of exploits both in the Bible and in the past and present generations, I have found out that prayer is a major key to success in every aspect of life.

Dr. Robert Schuller puts it this way; **"Through prayer God gives the power to hold on to tough times until the breakthrough comes. Prayer is the power that puts everything together successfully."**

Great men who known to have accomplished great exploits in life are not only dreamers, but they are also known for their excellent prayer lives. Also, if you check through the Bible, you will discover that men of exploits were men of prayer. Moses, Noah, Abraham, Isaac, Jacob, Gideon, Daniel, David, Peter, Paul, John and Jesus to mention but a few, were given to committed prayer on a daily basis and their success cannot be separated from their prayer lifestyles.

Friend, I don't know what your dream is, but I can tell you that you cannot bring it to reality on your own without getting connected to God in prayer.

Dr. David Oyedepo said; ***"You cannot fulfill a divine mandate in the energy of the flesh."***

Prayer is an art you have to learn and engage in consistently if the fulfillment of your dream is your desire.

Take Action In Faith

Hebrews 11:1-2, 6;

What is faith? It is the confident assurance that what we hope for is going to happen. It is the evidence of things we cannot yet see. God gave his approval to people in days of old because of their faith. So, you see, it is impossible to please God without faith. Anyone who wants to come to him must believe that there is a God and that he rewards those who sincerely seek him. (NLT)

Faith is a belief in the reality of your dream. Faith is the confident assurance that what you dream is real even though you cannot see it physically yet.

Please, understand that no man has ever fulfilled a dream on this earth without operating active faith for the reality of that dream. If you do not believe in the possibility of your dream, it is as good as not having any dream. Your faith in the possibility of that dream is what will cause a drive in your inner man towards its fulfillment. Your pursuit in life is simply a direct revelation of what you believe.

Faith is the greatest miracle working power in the world. No man can fail with faith. Failure at times is a product of unbelief. The beginning of faith is your belief in the idea that God has given you in form of a dream. If you do not believe it, you cannot become it. It is as simple as that.

Greatness in life depends not on a man's position; rather greatness does depend upon your belief in the positive ideas that flow into your imagination and your active pursuit of such ideas. That is what forms your dream.

Faith is the device through which you can lay hold on what God can do. Faith is the spiritual vital link between man and God so that man can realize what God can do. Faith is the foundation for the fulfillment of your dream and vision. That means the fulfillment of your dream in life is at the mercy of your own faith. Faith is so powerful that if well cultivated, it can move any mountain, break any barrier and obtain any desired result.

Faith is the ability to see the invisible, believe the unbelievable, dare the impossible and achieve the incredible. Faith always sees possibilities in the face of impossibilities

Look at how Jesus painted the picture in Mark 11:22-23;

And Jesus, replying, said to them, Have faith in God [constantly].

Truly I tell you, whoever says to this mountain, Be lifted up and thrown into the sea! and does not doubt at all in his heart but believes that what he says will take place, it will be done for him. (AMP)

Your faith is able to bring that dream to reality no matter how long you have conceived it. All you need is to put your faith on the line and believe strongly until you begin to see the fruit of your faith in the reality of your dream.

In another instance, Jesus emphasized the place of faith in achieving the impossible, in Matthew 17:20;

And Jesus said unto them, Because of your unbelief: for verily I say unto you, If ye have faith as a grain of mustard seed, ye shall say unto this mountain, Remove hence to yonder place; and it shall remove; and nothing shall be impossible unto you.

Your faith can move mountain so you need to take the step of faith to get you to your dream land. If you wait for everything to be alright before you take the step of faith, you cannot fulfill your dream.

In this world, one of the greatest lessons I have learnt is that nothing will ever be alright and perfect, but in the midst of imperfection, we must keep moving on by taking steps of faith towards our dream.

There are three aspects of faith that I want us to examine in the pursuit of our dreams; these are:

Your faith must in God. You must believe God for the release of His wisdom and divine strength that will help you as you move towards your dream.

Faith in God who is the giver of your dream is so crucial to your fulfillment. But the truth is that you get to know God by His word. And it is your knowledge of God that will determine your level of faith in Him and your level of faith in Him determines your level of exploits in life. Get to know

God by His Word from the Bible and other anointed materials (books, tapes etc.) by anointed men of God available to you.

Also, you need faith in your God-given ability. This is what is called self confidence. You must have confident assurance in the stuff you are made of. God has deposited great potential in you and he made you in His very image. Your understanding of the truth that there is the life of God in you will help you to believe in your God given ability and that will also help you a lot in the way you treat yourself which will determine the way others will treat you.

Norman Vincent Peale, The author of the legendary "Power of Positive Thinking" once said; ***"Believe in yourself! Have faith in your abilities! Without a humble but reasonable*** *confidence in your own powers you cannot be successful or happy."*

One thing that kills the potential miracle working power of faith is lack of self- confidence. That means if you do not believe in the great things that God can make happen through you, you cannot fulfill your dream.

No matter how small in status you may be, there are great possibilities in you.

If you see yourself as lacking ability to do something, you will never be able to do it.

You must get rid of that grasshopper mentality that makes you look like one in the eyes of the giants in the world. If you can see through the Word, the stuff God has made you, you will discover that you are also, a giant; a heavy weight champion. (See Numbers 13:33)

If you limit your choices only to what seems possible or reasonable, you disconnect yourself from what you truly want, and all that is left is a compromise. You cannot afford any compromise for self-limitation.

God has designed you to do great works that will impact the world. You are not ordinary; you are a representative of God on earth. You are born to reign and to overcome every challenge of life. You are made to be above all situations of life. You are full of the life of God. Your faith in this truth will go a long way to determine your level of accomplishment in life.

Again, your faith must have its source in God's Word. The source of faith is the Word of God. Romans 10:17; So then faith cometh by hearing, and hearing by the word of God.

Your faith in the Word of God and His power is very vital to your fulfillment in life. If you do not believe the Word of God, you cannot receive answers to your prayers, because your prayer must be based on what God has promised in his Word. God's Word is so powerful and it is a creative force. The world was formed or created by that creative force of the Word of God. The Word of God is not only creative in nature; it is prophetic and full of power. When you are glued to the Word of God, you will become superlatively creative and unlimitedly powerful. Your level of creativity is determined by your level of faith in the Word of God.

But how can you believe the Word that you are committed to? That is why Apostle Paul said in 2 Timothy 2:15;

Study to shew thyself approved unto God, a workman that needeth not to be ashamed, rightly dividing the word of truth.

Your approval is a direct product of your commitment to the study of God's Word. You must make the Word of God your daily bread. It is the food of the spirit man.

The best way to renew your mind is to read your bible every morning; your mind needs to be 'shampooed' with God's Word.

The Word of God is your access to strength that will keep you going in times of challenges and trials which are parts of the process of accomplishing your dream. Your faith can only grow as you constantly reason with God in His Word to determine your steps in this world in order to have your desires delivered. It is your faith that will bring you to the fulfillment of your dream must depend on the Word of God. Therefore, you must take action in faith in God, faith in your God given ability and faith in the Word of God as you stay committed to studying and obeying the Word.

Take Action In Giving

Your giving life has a lot to do in determining the fulfillment of your dream. How prepared you are to give of what you have determines how you can receive what you need from God and people to fulfill your dream.

Giving is one of the steps you need to take if you want to see the fulfillment of your dream. You might be thinking *"Why is he talking about giving in this book"?* Well, I am so much interested in the fulfillment of your dream that is why I do not want to leave any stone unturned in my bid to share the secret of fulfillment of dream with you.

Friend, if you are a student of biographies, you will discover that all great men are well known to be great givers. Giving of what you have will connect you to having what you do not have which you certainly need to fulfill your dream. It is part of the rule of the game.

Some people feel it's foolish to give unless you are getting something in return. That is not true giving, that is conditional giving. The real giving is selfless.

If you are not a giver, you cannot receive help from God and man and if you do not receive divine help, and the help of man, you may not get the required help needed to fulfill your dream.

Luke 6:38;

For if you give, you will get! Your gift will return to you in full and overflowing measure, pressed down, shaken together to make room for more, and running over. Whatever measure you use to give-large or small-will be used to measure what is given back to you. (TLB)

In other words, it is the value of what you give that determines the value of what you receive in return. Do not keep what you have to yourself alone, share with others. The more you give, the more you receive. Giving is the gateway to the fulfillment of your destiny. Your dream is a gift from God which will enable you to give value to people.

The more you share of what you have, the more it comes back to you; and it comes back greatly multiplied. Wealth that is shared creates more wealth. This principle is basic and it is a major course in the school of success. If you do not cultivate the habit of giving, you cannot be in a position to be blessed.

In this world there is a law that makes things work. That law is called the Law of seed time and harvest or the Law of giving and receiving. (See Genesis 8:22)

That Law simply means, there is a time of sowing and there is a time to reap what is sowed. If the time of sowing is sure and sowing is done, then the time of harvest is automatically sure.

Dr. Oral Robert once said; ***"As I sowed I'd reap, as I gave I'd receive, and every successful thing I accomplished started with a seed sown first. If you keep your seed and don't plant them, there will be no harvest. Give what you need to receive. Every time you give, you are ordering your harvest in advance. You can aim your seed to defeat your need."***

This great man is one of the most resourceful men in the world in his lifetime. That statement is part of the secrets that brought him into his greatness.

Cultivate a lifestyle of giving to God and people; making things happen in the kingdom of God and in the lives of people around you. These two forms of giving are important to your own fulfillment in life. The more valuables you give away, the more will come back to you in return. The more you help others to succeed, the more they will want to help you succeed.

It is more productive to give than to receive. Giving of money will produce the harvest of money. Giving of time to help people accomplish their dreams will produce the harvest of helps from people to fulfill your own dream (Acts 20:35)

Anytime you give, you are ordering your harvest in advance. When you give to God in form of tithes and offering, He opens a door of divine ideas to you. Creative ideas that will help you fulfill destiny will be opened to you as you give. Giving is one of the major channels by which God releases productive ideas to us. Do not take this for granted; give willingly, continuously, sacrificially and bountifully. That law is imperative for your fulfillment in life.

Make up your mind today to begin to sow seeds especially, financial seed, service seed, idea seed etc. to people, then you will begin to advance towards your fulfillment and successful accomplishment in life.

Take Action In Diligence

Diligence means hard work in the right direction. Until you take practical step to do the tasks involved in your dream, you cannot accomplish the object of that dream.

Since you have put down your plans and goals, you must create a daily agenda of work to be done to fulfill your dream and accomplish your goals. You cannot fulfill the dream that you do not pursue. Hard work is one of the major secrets of success. What you do not work for you cannot earn.

It was E.W. Kenyon that said; **"Dream, then carry out your dream. Drive yourself to the finish line; success belongs to the man who simply wills to do it."**

You have to carry out your dream by hard work. You have to drive yourself on a daily basis until you arrive at your destination which is the fulfillment of that dream. You must do something daily about your dream or else, you will not see it come true. You must fight for your dream everyday. There is no substitute for hard work. Success is not the result of luck or good fortune; it is rather a product of hard work and persistence. It might not be comfortable, but it is absolutely necessary to work hard and persist if you are really serious about winning and fulfilling your dream.

Labour is a major requirement for giving birth. If you are serious about giving birth to your success and the object of your dream, you must labour. There can be no bringing forth without labouring first. You cannot afford to wait on fortune. There is no guarantee in that, because any one who waits on fortune is never sure of dinner.

Roi Taner once said; *"You don't have to have money to be a successful business person. You don't need a college degree. You just need a lot of common sense backed up by a willingness to work hard."*

A willingness to work hard is a major the key to success. That is why Abraham Maslow, a Management School of Thought expert said; *"A musician must make music, an artist must make paint, a poet must write if he is to be ultimately at peace with himself. What one can be, one must be."*

Whatever you have discovered about yourself, you must work at it daily if it must become a reality. Hard work is the only way to attainment in life. No matter how little you can do daily, make sure you do something towards your dream. The greatest mistake in life is to do nothing because you can only do little.

It is a mistake not to do something, no matter how little as the Greek orator, Demosthenes puts it; **"Small opportunities are often the beginning of great enterprise."**

You have to work today if you desire a great tomorrow. Take that small step to work today and you will end up doing more on a daily basis. If you have a gift of writing, turn it to a business by looking for what you can write that will add value to humanity. Even if it is just a page to start with, just do it daily and as you do that you will improve and then become a renowned personality through your writings.

Many who are great authors today started very small. They have written books which are changing lives all over the world. The key is to do something about your dream daily. You cannot escape hard work if success is your desire.

You must be willing to accept responsibility as you take action in prayer, faith, giving and practical commitment with all diligence. It takes action to bring your dream to a reality. It is time to quit talking and start working.

Let me drive this point home by a statement made by the Greek philosopher; Aristotle, who said; *"In the arena of human life, the humours and rewards fall to those who show their good qualities in ACTION".*

Take action on your dream NOW!

Chapter 10: PATIENCE OF PURPOSE

Always bear in mind that your own resolution to succeed is more important than any other one thing.

ABRAHAM LINCOLN

People who can focus on one goal or dream or one business can be far more successful than those who try to do many things at once.

CONWAY STONE

"All dreams can come true...if we have the courage to pursue them."

WALT DISNEY

Determination is a major key for successful accomplishment. You have to be resolutely determined if you must turn your dream to reality. You must be doggedly determined to fulfill that dream or else you will tend to give up as a result of discouragement that will always come your way.

Life has its ways of testing every man, but if you are determined you will always pass the tests of life and overcome every form of discouragement. Winning belongs to those who are resolutely determined, come what may. And there has never been a winner who did not first expect to win. Great people are ordinary people with extraordinary amount of determination.

Some people gathered together one day and made a decision to do what had never been done before according to Bible record in Genesis Chapter 11. These people had a determination to build a tower that would reach heaven. Their determination was a product of their imagination. They were nearly successful in that project even though it was not a positive idea. Assuming the project was sanctioned by God, they would have succeeded as a result of their resolute determination. Your determination is a very powerful force that can change your life in no time.

When you determine that the thing can and shall be done, you will find the way, because the hardest rock will yield to those who drill with determination.

However, in this chapter, I will be showing you certain virtues that can boost your determination to succeed with your dream. I believe that your understanding of these virtues will help in giving more fire to your determination.

The Power of Expectation

Your expectation has power to determine what comes your way in life. If you are going to fulfill your dream, you must expect to win. Your fire of expectation must be burning high. Expectation is what gives birth to manifestation. No matter how big your dream is, how high your expectation to win is what will ultimately determine how successful you become in the race of life. Your attitude to life is the product of your expectation.

John C. Maxwell said; "When you change your expectation you change your attitude; when you change your attitude, you change your behaviour;

when you change your behaviour, you change your performance."

That statement simply shows that your performance in life is dictated by your expectation in life. Expectation of success will lead to success while expectation of failure will lead to failure.

I believe that the first and most important step toward success is the expectation that we can succeed in what we do. The reason is because you will see exactly what you expect to see in your life.

The great hero, Benjamin Franklin put it this way; **"Blessed is the one who expects nothing, for he shall receive it."**

Expectation is your hope of what will happen in your future. If what you hope to see negates what you dream to achieve, you may never achieve that dream, because what you expect does not correlate with what you dream. Your expectation is your hope and hope means; ***"Happy anticipation of good, eager longing, strained expectancy, watching with an outstretched head and abstraction from anything else that might engage the attention."***

Hope produces power pictures; inner pictures that faith builds on. Your hope must be red hot everyday. You can determine the change you desire through your expectation. Expect to win and you cannot but win in the race of life.

Sam Walton, the great business icon and founder of Wal-Mart Inc. once said; ***"High expectation is the key to everything."***

You must have high expectation in order to achieve great success with your dream.

The Power of Focus

Your focus is what holds your attention and if you must fulfill your dream, you must focus on the finishing line. You must get rid of all forms of distractions. You must set your eyes on what you want and fight for it. It is the end result that should hold your attention, because, it is what holds our attentions that determines our action. You may want to do a lot of things, but if you are serious about pursuing your dream, you must focus your efforts on one dream at a time. You are not likely going to be able to do too many things at the same time.

It is very important to note that those who have achieved great things in life are people of great focus who concentrated their efforts on one particular goal and once that was achieved, they moved on to the next one.

Through the power of focus, men in the past and present generations have achieved great and impactful feats that the world is still celebrating today.

However, if I mention certain names now, you will immediately connect them to one major thing that they are known with. For instance;

Isaac Newton	Law of Gravity
Michael Faraday	Electrolysis
Henry Ford	Automobile

Thomas Edison	Incandescent bulb
Bill Gates (Microsoft)	Computer Software
Steve Job	Apple Computer – iphone, ipod & ipad.
Alexander Graham Bell	Telephone
Sam Walton	Wal-Mart
Michael Jordan	Basketball
Diego Maradona	Football
Bill Cosby	Comedy
John C. Maxwell	Leadership
Ben Carson	Neurosurgery
McDonald	Burger

I have taken the time to list those names and what they are known with so that you can discover how powerful you can become when you focus your efforts on one object at a time.

John Mason asked this question in one of his books when he said; ***"If you could become famous for one thing in your life, what would it be?"***

You must be known for something; and my question to you is ***"What are you known for? What do you focus your efforts on? What is your concentration?"***

Until you are known for one particular thing, you are not likely to achieve success in life.

Please read the following statements from men of focus;

Every man has become great; every successful man has succeeded in proportion as he has confined his powers to one particular channel - Orison Swett Marden

The first law of success is concentration, to bend all the energies to one point and to go directly to that point, looking neither to the right nor to the left. - William Matthews

Concentrate all your thoughts on the task at hand. The sun's rays do not burn until brought to a focus. - Alexander Graham Bell

The Power of Courage

Courage is a major requirement in the school of successful accomplishment. There is no man who has fulfilled a dream without courage.

Courage is the inner strength that drives you on when your external circumstance seems contrary. Courage is a very crucial key to success in life.

The world is full of all manner of discouraging situations.

As a matter of fact, the appearance of things look discouraging, but you need to be strong and be very courageous as you follow your dream.

If you want to base your life on what your physical eyes can see in terms of challenges, you are not likely to fulfill your dream, because the physical condition is not always consistent with your dream. Courage is needed to arrive at your dream in spite of the negative situations.

God knows how important courage is in fulfilling any dream or vision and that is why He told Joshua repeatedly to be courageous in order to accomplish his divine tasks.

Joshua 1:6-7, 9;

BE STRONG AND OF A GOOD COURAGE: for unto this people shalt thou divide for an inheritance the land, which I sware unto their fathers to give them.

ONLY BE THOU STRONG AND VERY COURAGEOUS, that thou mayest observe to do according to all the law, which Moses my servant commanded thee: turn not from it to the right hand or to the left, that thou mayest prosper whithersoever thou goest.

Have not I commanded thee? BE STRONG AND OF A GOOD COURAGE; be not afraid, neither be thou dismayed: for the LORD thy God is with thee whithersoever thou goest.

Can you see how God was emphasizing the need for Joshua to be strong and courageous? You and I need courage to conquer all challenges on our way to fulfilling our dreams in life. If you lack courage you will faint in the pursuit of your dream.

You need to learn how to encourage yourself by speaking loud your possibilities. You can draw great inspiration for courage as you study the Word of God and read the stories of men who have accomplished great feats against all odds.

Another way to encourage yourself is to celebrate every step you take towards your dream, no matter how little. If you can do anything that moves you toward your dream, it is worth celebrating. And as you do, you will gain more courage to do more and more until you arrive at the fulfillment of your dream.

Also, when the going gets tough, the tough will always get going, and tough times do not always last, only people who are tough actually do. It takes a courageous person to keep going when the going gets tough. As long as you have something you are pursuing, things will not come easily. There will be situations that look like setbacks, but courage is what you need to turn your setbacks to a set up for a come back.

You have to be courageously tough if you want to fulfill your dream in life. Some times, circumstances will whisper to you that what you are pursuing is not possible. You will sometimes see what others have achieved and feel like you cannot do it, but the truth is that you can do even more than them. All you need is to be courageous and bold in your actions towards your dream. When you understand that life has its own testing times, you will develop courage to go through the tests and come out refined as gold.

Walt Disney once said; **"All our dreams can come true if we have the courage to pursue them."**

In other words, it takes courage to see a dream come true. Men of exploits are men of courage. You are a man of exploits, so you must possess this virtue of courage which will take you to your dreamland. All the great dreamers I have written about would not have been able to reach the fullness of their dreams without the fire of courage burning in them. These men *"failed"* several times, but they never saw it as failure. They kept reaching higher and higher in the midst of their purported failure until they hit the mark of their dreams.

You too can do it. You can fulfill that dream. All you need is to be courageous and move on, no matter what obstacles you meet on the way. Your success or failure in fulfilling your dream will be determined by your courage. It is courage that will help you overcome adversities and challenges of life.

Proverbs 24:10;

If thou faint in the day of adversity, thy strength is small.

Your courage is your strength and to avoid fainting in the day of adversity, you must build up your strength which is your courage.

The secrets of men are in their stories. David in the bible as you know the story was a man of unusual courage.

1 Samuel 30:6;

And David was greatly distressed; for the people spake of stoning him, because the soul of all the people was grieved, every man for his sons and for his daughters: but David encouraged himself in the LORD his God.

David was a great warrior who operated with the secret of self encouragement. He constantly encouraged himself in the Lord. He faced a lot of battles and he won all by taking advantage of the virtue of courage.

I believe that you too can encourage yourself in the Lord who gave you that dream, and as you do, you will surely get to the finishing line.

The Power of Patience

Every great dreamer in the world possesses this great virtue called patience. No matter how big and great your dream is, without patience, you cannot fulfill it. You must learn how to wait for the fulfillment of your dream. You cannot see the reality of the object of your dream immediately. You must be patient not to jeopardize the reality of your dream by impatience.

Dreamers are like farmers and every successful farmer understands the importance of patience in reaping of their crops. They know that there is need to wait for their crops to become ripe enough before they harvest them.

No farmer goes to farm to plant crops and expects to harvest it next day. There is need for time to be given to the crops to germinate and grow well until the harvest time. There is a seed time and there is a harvest time. If any farmer does not wait for the harvest time before he goes to harvest his crops, he has wasted the seed and the time spent in planting. It is not harvest that immediately follows seed planting, it is time. The time to wait requires a lot of patience. Every precious seed needs the required time to become a bountiful harvest.

This is the way it works for your dream as well. This key is a missing link in the race of life. Many dreams have died or been aborted as a result of the impatience of the dreamer because they could not wait for the right time required for their dream-seed to mature enough to become tangible fruits.

Dr. Mike Murdock said; **"Expect your seed of patience to produce a harvest. Every dreamer must tolerate a season of waiting and waiting is not a wasted time."**

The season of waiting is a must for every dream to come though. There is no short cut to success in life; waiting is part of the process.

There is need to cultivate the attitude of patience because it will determine your ability to keep your hope alive and be on course with your eyes focused on the end result of your dream.

Friend, I believe you sincerely desire to fulfill your dream. And no matter how big and great that dream is, and no matter how you have followed the necessary steps in the pursuit of that dream, the place of patience cannot be over emphasized if it must become a reality. No matter how slow your motion may appear, with patience, even the snail made it to the ark and the patient dog eats the fattest bone. You will get to your success and the best of God is reserved for you if only you are patient.

If you possess the virtues of expectation, focus, courage with patience, your determination to succeed cannot be stopped. Your dream has great possibilities, so keep fighting for its fulfillment.

Dream lofty dreams, and as you dream, so shall you become. Your vision is the promise of what you shall one day be. Your Ideal is the prophecy of what you shall at last unveil.

JAMES ALLEN

PART THREE

BARRIERS TO THE FULFILMENT OF DREAM

The first part of this book revealed to us what dreams are while the second part helps to know what to do to fulfill our dreams in life.

However, in this third part, I will be sharing with you the enemies that stand in the way of every dreamer. These enemies are surmountable. Every dreamer who has accomplished their dreams faced these enemies and they overcame them. This is because, until you understand these enemies and set yourself to get rid of them, you may still not be able to get to the destination of your dream.

Please understand that the journey of success is full of what to do and what not to do. The equation must be balanced before you can successfully accomplish the objects of your dream. There are things to do and there are things not to do or things to guard against.

As you take the time to study this part and decide to overcome these enemies, I see you get to your desired dreamland with speed. It is your turn to be celebrated as you fulfill your dream.

Chapter 11: FEAR

How much pains have cost us the evils which have never happened!

THOMAS JEFFERSON

One of the greatest discoveries a man makes; one of his great surprises; is to find he can do what he was afraid he couldn't do.

HENRY FORD

You don't overcome fear; you embrace it and walk through your doubts, knowing you have the capacity to achieve your dream inspite of your fears; because fear is False Expectations Appearing Real.

FARRAH GRAY

Fear is one of the major reasons why many people failed to follow their dreams in order to turn them to reality. But the truth is there are always things that will make you afraid in the journey of life, but if you study life very carefully, you will discover that most of the things you are afraid of never happen. There is no reason strong enough for you not to fulfill your dream, no matter what you call it. Everybody feels fear, but the feeling of fear is a proof that you can do what you are afraid of.

If you are afraid of taking risks, you cannot fulfill your dream, because there are necessary risks that must be taken to achieve success in life.

Everyone who has accomplished any great thing in life took some dangerous, but calculated risks before they got there.

Dr. Myles Munroe once said; **"Do not be afraid to fail. You will never succeed greatly until you are willing to fail greatly. It is better to have tried and failed than to not have tried and never know you could have succeeded."**

If you are afraid of failure, you cannot fulfill your dream. Fear of failure will keep you from taking necessary risks. The fear of failure keeps people in the box and until you take steps to get out of the box, you remain locked up in the box. When you learn how to do the thing you are afraid of, the death of fear is sure. That is one of the surest ways to deal with fear.

People who have never experienced failure usually don't accomplished much. Only those are not afraid of sinking can step out to walk on the water.

Vince Lombardi, a legendary Football coach said; **"If you can't accept losing, you can't win. It is not whether you get knocked down; it is whether you get up again."**

Failure is not the inability to accomplish what you want at the time you want it, rather, failure is a decision not to try again. If you get knocked down and you decided not to go again, then you have failed. But as long as you are still pressing, you cannot be termed a failure in life, because you will soon get there as long as you keep going.

The fear that stops people from fulfilling their dream is of different kinds. There is the fear of failure, fear of making mistake, fear of the unknown, fear of rejection, fear of taking risk et cetera. However, it is your responsibility to get rid of whatever kind of fear that stands in your way of fulfillment.

Fear is a spirit and it is from the devil who does not want you to fulfill your dream. The enemy is always after your dream, because the fulfillment of your dream will lead to solutions to people's problems and your enemy does not want that to happen.

2 Timothy 1:7;

For God hath not given us the spirit of fear; but of power, and of love, and of a sound mind.

The gifts of God in you did not include fear. Fear is not from God. From the scripture above, it is made clear that fear is a spirit and the major way to fight the spirit of fear is to possess the spirit of faith. And as a child of God, made in His image, you have that spirit of faith in you. All you need is to use it to defeat that spirit of fear that stands in your way of fulfillment.

2 Corinthians 4:13;

We having the same spirit of faith, according as it is written, I believed, and therefore have I spoken; we also believe, and therefore speak.

You have the spirit of faith in you; therefore, fear cannot hold you to ransom.

I read from one great author who said; ***"When fear knocks at the door of your heart, send faith to open it and you will discover that nothing is at the door."***

The phrase; do not fear or don't be afraid appears in the Bible about 365 times according to bible scholars. That means there is a ***"do not fear"*** tablet for you every morning as you study the Word of God.

If you will be committed to receiving counsels from the Spirit of God every morning by studying the Word of God, you will discover that the spirit of faith in you will become stronger and you will never know what fear means any more. You will hear the Spirit of God telling you ***"fear not, take the risk, move forward, and go ahead"***.

Every visionary is known to be a risk taker, because, it is the ability to take well calculated risks that makes you an influence in the world.

John C. Maxwell said; ***"The greatest mistake we make is living in constant fear that we will make one."***

The world is a battle ground and you must fight for your dream by taking the risk and as you do, you will deal with fear. It's time for you not only to get ready but to live ready and fight to win. You have what it takes to win in the battles confronting you on the way to the fulfillment of your dream.

Wake up and fight for your dream because it is worth fighting for. Refuse to fear failure, rejection, criticisms, and all the likes.

Take action now and move out of the box that you have stayed all these years as a result of fear, so that you do not end up in the box of unfufillment.

No matter how dark things seem to be or actually are, raise your sights and see the possibilities – always see them, for they're always there.

NORMAN VINCENT PEALE

Chapter 12: PROCRASTINATION

Foolish people procrastinate. They put off acting on their ideas.

ROBBERT SCHULLER

A common quality of successful, happy people is that they are action oriented. When they hear a good idea, they take action on it immediately to see if it can help them.

BRIAN TRACY

Do your work. Not just your work and no more, but a little more for the lavishing sake - that little more that is worth all the rest.

DEAN BRIGGS

One of the greatest enemies of destiny is procrastination. Many people's dreams have died today as a result of this dangerous enemy. There is no way any one who indulges continuously in the act of procrastination can fulfill a dream.

The truth is that, the more you procrastinate on the tasks involved in your dream, the farther away you are from the fulfillment of that dream. That is why it is not every dream that gets to the stage of fulfillment, many have died prematurely.

If you are going to fulfill you dream, you must get rid of that attitude of procrastination, because, the vision you do not act upon, the object you cannot accomplish.

When you possess the attitude of prompt action, it can affect every phase of your life. It can help you do the things you should do but do not feel like doing. Also, it can keep you from procrastinating when an unpleasant duty faces you, but it can also help you do those things that you want to do. It will help you seize those precious moments that, if lost, may never be retrieved.

What is procrastination?

Procrastination can be defined in the following ways:

-to put off intentionally the doing of something that should be done, to postpone or delay needlessly, to put off till another day or time; defer; delay, putting off or delaying or deferring an action to a later time, act of delaying; inactivity resulting in something being put off until a later time, slowness as a consequence of not getting around to it

However, in psychology, procrastination refers to the act of replacing high-priority actions with tasks of low-priority, and thus putting off important tasks to a later time. In other words, procrastination is not absolute inaction in most cases and it is not laziness, rather, it is delayed action or acting on unimportant issues. It is concentration of valuable time and efforts in a wrong task.

That simply means, procrastinating does not connote doing absolutely nothing. Procrastinators seldom do absolutely anything; rather, they do marginally useful things leaving the most important things undone.

I believe that there are many things you ought to have done years back which were very important to your fulfillment in life, but you kept putting them off till later. And that 'later' has not come till now. You kept saying; "I know what I need to do", but you have not taken the step to do it. That is not to say that you are not doing some other things, but that very important thing has been left unattended.

Most times you think you are waiting patiently for the right time to do what is important, well, it is good to be patient, but if you look inward, you will discover that in a lot of cases as it relates to what you need to do, inaction is not being patient, rather it is procrastination.

By now, many people's dreams should have seen the light of day, but it is still in the incubator probably because they keep delaying certain very important actions till later time and that delayed action has led to delay in fulfillment of their dreams.

Don Marquis once said; **"Procrastination is the art of keeping up with yesterday."**

When you put off very important and most pressing actions towards your dream till later time for whatever reason, all you are doing is keeping up with yesterday. And you cannot make any meaningful progress with that attitude.

Procrastination steals the valuable time you have to do most valuable things. It has the capacity of making one a foot-dragger; because, it is actually an act of foot dragging. Accept the fact that there simply is not enough time to do everything. That is why it is so important to work on the most important things. If you are always focused on the important things, both in your business and personal life, you will always be making the greatest contribution by using your time wisely.

It was Lord Chesterfield who said; **"Know the true value of time; snatch, seize, and enjoy every moment of it. No idleness, no laziness, and no procrastination: never put off till tomorrow what you can do today."**

As you read this book, I am sure that you have already seen certain things that you ought to have done years past which you have not done because you kept putting it off till tomorrow. If you will do a proper assessment of where you are now and where you should have been by taking action on those things years ago, you will know that you are far behind in the pursuit of your dream. You might have a way of consoling yourself by saying; "it is not late to do it". But I think it is better to have done it on time and at a younger age, so that you can move to the next dream of your life, than to have lost the fervor required in getting it done by virtue of time dynamics.

John C. Maxwell, a renowned Leadership Coach once said; **"Good executives never put off until tomorrow what they can get someone else to do today."**

Perhaps, by now at least about One Million people should have read your dream book, which still remains a dream. And as a matter of fact, out of that number, many should have discovered from that book great dreams that would have made them become solutions to this world. But as long as that book remains a dream, it cannot be a solution to the world, since it did not become a reality.

God expects you to act on your dream without any further delay. Stop foot-dragging, take action. Now is the time because it is the right time.

Additionally, procrastination makes people become unstable and excellence is impossible with instability.

That was the lifestyle of Reuben in Genesis 49:3-4;

Reuben, thou art my firstborn, my might, and the beginning of my strength, the excellency of dignity, and the excellency of power:

UNSTABLE AS WATER, THOU SHALT NOT EXCEL...

Reuben was the first born, the beginning of his father's strength. He was the excellency of dignity and power, yet he was told by his father that he would not excel, because he was unstable as water. That is one of the dangers of procrastination. It stops people from attaining excellence in life.

Several reasons have been identified as the causes of procrastination and these include:

Fear

This could be fear of mistake, fear of failure, fear of rejection, fear of the unknown, fear of taking risk etc. No matter the kind of fear you may be having, you can deal with it. All you need is focus on the goal you have set to achieve and the strength to get rid of the fear will come.

Also, you must develop the spirit of boldness by the help of the Holy Spirit and fear will never have effect on your life.

Anxiety

You have no reason to be anxious, because anxiety has a way of turning you to a procrastinator. You need to get rid of anxiety if you want to fulfill your dream. And you have an assurance of a great future in God as you make Him your dream partner. He knows tomorrow and He will take you step by step to that great future as you walk with Him.

Philippians 4:6-7;

DO NOT BE ANXIOUS ABOUT ANYTHING, but in everything, by prayer and petition, with thanksgiving, present your requests to God.

And the peace of God, which transcends all understanding, will guard your hearts and your minds in Christ Jesus. (NIV)

The resultant effect of an anxiety-free life is peace that is beyond human understanding. When you have peace about your dream, you will not procrastinate.

Low Self Worth Or Self Defeating Mentality

When you lose sight of your personal worth or your identity, you will develop a low self worth or self esteem which will degenerate into a self defeating mentality. And with a self defeating mentality, you will keep putting off certain most important steps that you are supposed to take in fulfilling your dream.

As a matter of fact, self defeating mentality will hinder you from taking giant strides which are needed in most cases to fulfilling your dream. What picture do you hold of yourself? How do you assess your worth in God? It is the picture you hold of yourself that will determine your actions in life. If you are small in your own eyes, you will not dare big things.

Proverbs 23:7;

For as he thinketh in his heart, so is he...

You must change the picture you hold of yourself if it is not consistent with what God has revealed in His Word about you. There is nothing as important in your life as your mental attitude towards yourself, what you think of yourself, the model which you hold of yourself and your possibilities. If your mental attitude toward yourself is self defeating, the chances of you achieving great things are very low. Therefore, you need to see yourself the way God sees you.

How To Turn Procrastination To A Positive Tool For Fulfillment of Your Dream

One major key to turning procrastination to a tool of accomplishment of your dream is to practice Creative or Structured procrastination.

As I earlier noted, procrastination is not inaction, rather it is mostly acting on less important tasks while the most important ones are left unattended.

Creative or Structured procrastination is a swap from procrastinating on most important tasks to procrastinating on less important tasks. It is leaving the less valuable tasks unattended while actions and efforts are centered on most valuable tasks that help in fulfilling ones dream.

To practice Creative or Structured procrastination is to get busy on the most important tasks relating to the fulfillment of your dream while you procrastinate on the less important ones.

For instance, you have a dream of writing and publishing a book. There are many tasks involved in fulfilling that dream while there are many other tasks you could get involved in which many not necessarily be required for fulfilling the book writing and publishing dream.

As an author, I know that you cannot be a successful author without making references to others who have accomplished the things you are trying to accomplish in fulfilling your dream. Therefore, a commitment to reading of relevant materials everyday is part of the most important tasks involved in fulfilling writing and publishing dream.

Additionally, you need to do a lot of thinking and meditating on issues relating to the subject of the book you are writing.

All these are very important, top on the list tasks involved in the pursuit of your dream as an author.

However, there are other tasks that call for your attention everyday which may not necessarily be needed in the fulfillment of your dream. Those are tasks that are considered less important on your list.

To follow your dream effectively, practicing Creative or Structured procrastination is an attitude you need to develop. You need to learn the art of prioritizing your priorities. In other words, you must place high priority on most important tasks which will help you in fulfilling your dream while low priority is placed on less important tasks.

Prioritize the list of what you need to do according to importance in your assessment. The easiest way to do this is to categorize each item into three major sections:

A) Crucial and Urgent

B) Important but Not As Urgent

C) Neither Important Nor Urgent.

The A's are the most important and therefore should take top priority-- always. B's are next in line and C's are seldom worth spending your time on.

Taking the time to prioritize in the beginning will help you to knock off one task after another, without stopping to decide the relevant importance of a task.

Therefore, to successfully practice Creative or Structured procrastination, you need to take action on most important tasks or those of high priority everyday and procrastinate on less important tasks or those of low priority.

You can fulfill your dream because you have what it takes to get it done. Prompt action on high priority tasks is the key to dealing with the enemy called procrastination.

Also, introduce creativity into how you go about the pursuit of your dream and you will discover that it does not really take time; rather, it takes prompt action with wisdom.

Chapter 13: PRIDE

The fear of the LORD is to hate evil: pride, and arrogancy, and the evil way, and the froward mouth, do I hate.

PROVERBS 8:13

When men are most sure and arrogant they are commonly most mistaken, giving views to passion without that proper deliberation which alone can secure them from the grossest absurdities.

DAVID HUME

Nobody can be as amusingly arrogant as a young man who has just discovered an old idea and thinks it is his own.

SYDNEY J. HARRIS

Fulfillment of dream is impossible with the attitude of pride and arrogance. Many whose dreams have been hindered from fulfillment are either proud or arrogant; claiming to know what they do not actually know.

Proud and arrogant people do not have respect for the counsel of other people, especially those who have accomplished what they dream of accomplishing.

In this dreamers' world, the proud and arrogant are not reckoned with as men of greatness, because; humility is the price for greatness. Acknowledgment of the help of God in everything we do is a proof of our humility. And when we express our gratitude to God for His help in accomplishing our dream phase by phase, He will release more of His help to us for the accomplishment of greater things in the pursuit of our dreams.

James 4:6;

But he giveth more grace. Wherefore he saith, God resisteth the proud, but giveth grace unto the humble.

The bottom line is that everything we have is a gift from God. Arrogant people have trouble acknowledging this. They did not want to accept that God has helped them, because they feel it will minimize the impact of their accomplishments.

Next time you feel pride in a natural ability; ask yourself, 'Did I do anything to earn it?' or 'Did I control all the circumstances that put me in the right place at the right time to get this fantastic opportunity?'

Ego is nothing but pride in its inflated form. Arrogance is an absorbing sense of one's own greatness. It is a feeling of one's superiority over others. In the presence of superiors, overweening pride manifests itself as arrogance.

Pride is a haughty attitude shown by somebody who believes, often unjustifiably, that he or she is better than others. Also, pride will always stand in the way of further development. In other words, the proud will be limited in personal growth and self development which should help in achieving more results than the previous.

It is common to become arrogant about the things we achieve through hard work, because a person really feels like he **"did it."** But no one can do anything without the help of God, no matter how hard one can work or how intelligent one may be.

One of the ways to guard against pride is to be grateful for the insights you have had, and to the people who have helped you along the way. It is important for us to know that, we could never achieve anything without our parents and teachers, and without those who have blazed the trail before us. It is good to enjoy your accomplishments, but not to the point of thinking that those things make you superior to other people.

Arrogant people are overbearing. They have little patience for those who do not exhibit the same level of achievement. It is to behave in ways that do not consider truths outside itself. It is overbearing pride; exaggerated self-opinion; too great confidence in one's self.

Arrogance is the aspiration of lowness to knowledge of life. It is about one's goodness is the most dangerous, because it is in the name of 'goodness' that many of the world's most evil acts are performed. It is when you look down on others. Watch out, so that you do not destroy others on your path to accomplishment.

Pride is one of the biggest obstacles to attaining wisdom. If you are arrogant, it is impossible to learn from others. Pride leads to contempt; gratitude leads to compassion. Be grateful to your teachers. It's arrogant to say: 'This is simple. I knew it all along.' If someone is spending time teaching you, acknowledge his effort - whether or not you think you've learned something.

Again, people make the mistake of thinking that they have to trumpet or broadcast their success in order to feel good about it. But in fact, not taking credit often results in a better feeling, because this way you do good simply because it is good, not for the fame it earns you. If you are busy patting yourself on the back for what you have achieved, you will not make an effort to do more. And that will hinder the full realization of your dream.

Also, if you are constantly defending your opinions, you will never be open to hearing new ideas, and new ideas are always needed to accomplish more results in life. Therefore, to be arrogant about your ideas is to keep limiting yourself.

Pride is a limiting factor. It places a limit on man's destiny. When you allow pride to set in, it will stop you from achieving more, because; it will hinder the release of your potential. Pride leads to a fall and destruction.

Proverbs 16:18-19;

Pride goeth before destruction, and an haughty spirit before a fall.

Better it is to be of an humble spirit with the lowly, than to divide the spoil with the proud.

Pride is an enemy to the fulfillment of your dream; you must do all you have to do to fight against it as you seek to bring your dream to reality. When you get to the point where you think you can do it all alone, without the help of God and other people, you should know that pride has begun to set in. At that point, go to God in prayer, asking Him to take away that spirit of pride from your life.

Even Jesus, the Christ affirmed that He could not get any result without God and the people around Him.

John 5:30;

I can of mine own self do nothing: as I hear, I judge: and my judgment is just ; because I seek not mine own will, but the will of the Father which hath sent me.

We need to accept the truth that we cannot fulfill any dream without God.

John 15:5;

I am the vine, ye are the branches: He that abideth in me, and I in him, the same bringeth forth much fruit: for without me ye can do nothing.

It very important to reject pride and arrogance so that you will gain access to divine help that will enable you to fulfill your dream. Remember that you need to appreciate the people that God surrounds you with as they are needed for the fulfillment of your dream. This is how you can overcome pride in your bid to fulfill your dream.

Chapter 14: SELF-CENTEREDNESS

When a man is wrapped up in himself he makes a pretty small package.

JOHN RUSKIN

The greatest achievements are those that benefit others.

DENIS WAITLEY

If you think about what you ought to do for people, your character will take care of itself.

WOODROW WILSON

There is no one who has ever fulfilled a dream in life who is self-centered. This attitude is a major enemy in the pursuit of greatness. As you know that your dream is expected to bring you into greatness, but there is no one who can become great with the attitude of self-centeredness. That is why this enemy must be avoided in your bid to fulfill your dream.

Self-centeredness means, thinking only of self, tending to concentrate selfishly on your own needs and affairs and to show little or no interest in those of others.

The object of your dream is supposed to make you a blessing to people, no matter what it is. If you have a dream that is focused on yourself alone, it is self-centered and therefore, cannot become a reality as far as God is concerned. A self-centered dream is the same as selfish ambition which does not have the capacity to last because God has no respect for any form of selfish ambition.

In all my years of study about the subject of greatness, I have discovered that every great and big dream is people-focused and others-centered. Small dream focuses on self, while big dream focuses on others. There is no way a selfish dream can obtain divine help from God for fulfillment.

Self-centeredness is typically viewed as the most unappealing personality trait in a potential friend or partner. Most of us struggle to maintain a sense of compassion and understanding toward others. Self-centered people, on the other hand, do not bother to take the time to understand another person's point-of-view or feelings.

When you are self-centered, you will not learn from others. And if you do not learn from others, your view about life will be very limited.

Also, real and effective leadership springs from a heart willing and ready to serve. A leader does not boss over people; rather, he serves people by influencing them to fulfill their God given purpose and dream on earth. Great leaders are actually servants of the people they lead. They do not exercise lordship and authority over people. They use their God given dream, potential and privileges to serve the people. They are not living for self; rather they are living to serve.

There is a parable of Jesus about a man with a selfish dream recorded in Luke 12:16-20;

And he spake a parable unto them, saying, The ground of a certain rich man brought forth plentifully:

And he thought within himself, saying, What shall I do, because I have no room where to bestow my fruits?

And he said, This WILL I DO: I WILL PULL DOWN MY BARNS, AND BUILD GREATER; AND THERE WILL I BESTOW ALL MY FRUITS AND MY GOODS.

And I WILL SAY TO MY SOUL, SOUL, THOU HAST MUCH GOODS LAID UP FOR MANY YEARS; TAKE THINE EASE, EAT, DRINK, AND BE MERRY.

But God said unto him, Thou fool, this night thy soul shall be required of thee: then whose shall those things be, which thou hast provided?

This story actually reveals to us that self-centeredness is a practical demonstration of foolishness. This rich man had a very good dream of business expansion. I believe that a dream of expansion in our businesses is a God-ordained and positive dream. But the intention or motive behind such expansion is what determines the outcome of such dream.

A dream that will not make you serve other people will starve you to death, just as the case of the rich fool. God who is the source of your dream does not want you to live for self; rather He wants you to live for others.

Self-centeredness is a limiting factor standing on the road to man's destiny. It is very important to fight against it.

Philippians 2:3-4;

Do nothing from factional motives [through contentiousness, strife, selfishness, or for unworthy ends] or prompted by conceit and empty arrogance. Instead, in the true spirit of humility (lowliness of mind) LET EACH REGARD THE OTHERS AS BETTER THAN AND SUPERIOR TO HIMSELF [THINKING MORE HIGHLY OF ONE ANOTHER THAN YOU DO OF YOURSELVES].

LET EACH OF YOU ESTEEM AND LOOK UPON AND BE CONCERNED FOR NOT

[MERELY] HIS OWN INTERESTS, BUT ALSO EACH FOR THE INTERESTS OF OTHERS. (AMP)

Apostle Paul, a man of great visions from God was known to have lived for the wellbeing of others. He ended up a fulfilled man. From his statement above, it is not out of place to conclude that, living for others is the real life.

Whenever we insist on having "our own way", we are acting completely antithetically to the revealed character of Jesus, the great dreamer of God's salvation plan for mankind. A self-centered lifestyle therefore is an anomaly, a gross abnormality and a monstrous perversion. It is completely incompatible with a genuine followership of the Lord Jesus Christ and other great dreamers.

Kate Halverson once said; **"If you are all wrapped up in yourself, you are over dressed."**

Learning from the example of Jesus, it is so clear that He was not wrapped up in Himself. He was always longing for solution to people's problems. As a matter of fact, His dream for humanity was for every man to become what God ordained them to become. He chose to suffer for mankind to enjoy life. He chose to fast for mankind to eat well and finally, He chose to die for mankind to live.

Philippians 2:5-8

Let this mind be in you, which was also in Christ Jesus:

Who, being in the form of God, thought it not robbery to be equal with God:

BUT MADE HIMSELF OF NO REPUTATION, AND TOOK UPON HIM THE FORM OF A SERVANT, AND WAS MADE IN THE LIKENESS OF MEN:

And being found in fashion as a man, he humbled himself, and became obedient unto death, even the death of the cross.

However, it is a well known fact that human nature is naturally selfish. But following Jesus' example by having His kind of heart, according to the statement of Paul in that scriptural passage above, we can deal with self-centeredness.

Also, being filled with the Holy Spirit is another major way by which we can deal with self-centeredness. We must seek to be filled with the Holy Spirit from time to time so that self can be dethroned while God is enthroned. And when we enthrone God in our lives, a heart for others will replace a self-centered attitude in us.

This is a major truth to uphold in our bid to fulfill our God-given dream. We must fight against this enemy called self-centeredness.

Chapter 15: IMPATIENCE

"Learn the art of patience. Apply discipline to your thoughts when they become anxious over the outcome of a goal. Impatience breeds anxiety, fear, discouragement and failure. Patience creates confidence, decisiveness, and a rational outlook, which eventually leads to success".

BRIAN ADAMS

He who can have patience can have what he wills.

BENJAMIN FRANKLIN

Impatience aborts destiny. It leads to poor performance which results into failure in accomplishing the objects of a dream. It is an enemy that must be dealt with as soon as it is noticed.

In chapter ten, I discussed about how powerful patience is, the joy of having the virtue of patience and the danger of not having it in our bid to bring our dreams to reality. However, in this chapter, I will dwell on impatience and how it can hinder you from fulfilling your dream.

First of all, let us define patience as endurance, perseverance. It means waiting in faith for the reality of what you believe God for while you are busy working towards it.

Another word for patience is long suffering which is one of the fruits of the spirit. In other words, patience is a virtue of the Holy Spirit. It can also be described as forbearance. Also, patience is the ability to wait till the end; refusing to quit or faint in the pursuit of your purpose, vision, dream and assignment in life.

Hebrews 12:1;

Wherefore seeing we also are compassed about with so great a cloud of witnesses, let us lay aside every weight, and the sin which doth so easily beset us, and LET US RUN WITH PATIENCE THE RACE THAT IS SET BEFORE US.

Your God-given dream is the race set before you by God to run, but your must know what is required of you to run the race.

It is so unfortunate that we are in a generation plagued with *"I want it now"* syndrome. Also, the blessing of technology has made the people of this generation forget that due process is ordained of God for any great thing to be accomplished. Are we forgetting the fact that, God is a God of times and seasons? (Ecclesiastes 3:1)

Technology cannot change God; neither can it change His operations. For instance, the gestation period for a pregnant woman is nine months ever since the world began and it has not changed. If any pregnant woman goes to deliver at the fifth month of pregnancy, that will be a premature birth which in most cases leads to a stillbirth and the death of the mother, except by divine intervention. If the mother can wait patiently for three more months according to the time of life, there will be a safe delivery of the baby with the mother alive and well.

Many a great dream in the heart of man is aborted as premature leading to a stillbirth as a result of impatience. If you want to have a successful delivery of your dream, you must be patient for the right time after the gestation period. You must leave the company of the ***"I want it now" and move to the company of the "I will wait until the right time"***.

We must know that every of God's program in life is in phases. He takes us through life phase by phase. This is because we are to live by faith in Him and faith in God requires patience as we must believe Him for every phase in order to move to the next phase in the fulfillment of our dream.

As you are doing God's will, you need to be patient till you begin to see result. If you are impatient, you will not experience the reality of God's plan for your life as it relates to the fulfillment of your God-given dream.

This is because; God's program for us speaks at the end. That is why Jesus admonished that only those who endure till the end shall be saved.

Mark 13:13;

And ye shall be hated of all men for my name's sake: but HE THAT SHALL ENDURE UNTO THE END, the same shall be saved.

It is impatience that makes man to be in a hurry to accomplish his dream. Great dreams do not get fulfilled fast and quick as you will snap a picture with your camera. Everyone reputed for great accomplishment are dreamers with the virtue of patience. They have learnt how to deal with the impatient nature of man.

Many a great evil in the world today is largely as a result of impatience. A young man with a great dream of becoming wealthy goes into armed robbery, drug pushing, kidnapping or cyber crimes. All these happened because he is impatient to work on building a business that will bring him into wealth. In as much as a dream of becoming wealthy is not evil in itself; nevertheless some activities involved in the pursuit of that dream may be evil as a result of impatience.

God has ordained that His vision for us will speak at the end as we pursue it. His vision is likened to a seed planted which brings forth fruit in due season. (Habakkuk 2:3, James 5:7-11, Luke 8:15)

God has an appointed time for every of His children. The great future He has ordained for us requires our patience and perseverance to get there. His agenda for each of us delivers little by little and phase by phase. Our understanding of this will help us walk patiently until we arrive at our individual destination, which is the fulfillment of our dream. (Exodus 23:29-30)

One wise man said; *"With patience, even the snail made it to the ark."*

As slow as the snail is, it was part of the creature preserved by God in the time of Noah, because He was patient enough for the snail to get to the ark.

Some years back, I read this story about Macadamia nut tree; ***"When macadamia nut trees are cultivated, the first year, the tree looks like it won't live. The second year, it really looks terrible; and the third year, it looks like it should be dug up and burned. The fourth and fifth years are not much better. But at the sixth year, the tree begins bearing fruits and it continues to bear fruits for up to one hundred years."***

This is a very powerful illustration of the place of patience in the pursuit of our dream. There is no substitute for patience in the race of life. If the man who planted that nut tree had been impatient, he might have given up on it after third, fourth or fifth year. And if he gives up on it, he has lost a hundred years of harvest without yearly planting.

It was Arnold Glasow that said; **"The key to everything is patience. You get the chicken by hatching the egg, not by smashing it."**

If you smash the egg, you have lost the chicken. In other words, if you give up on your dream, you have lost the glory of its fulfillment. The best of this world has been reserved for you. All you need is to dream big, add patience to it as you deal with that human nature of impatience through the help of the Spirit.

You will not fail to accomplish your dream as you refuse to give up because of impatience.

THE FINAL WORD

BEGIN RIGHT NOW

"If your dream dies, dream another one. If things don't work out the way you've planned, God has a better plan for you".

JOEL OSTEEN

"The strongest oak of the forest is not the one that is protected from the storm and hidden from the sun. It's the one that stands in the open where it is compelled to struggle for its existence against the winds and rains and the scorching sun. Effort only fully releases its reward after a person refuses to quit."

NAPOLEON HILL

"The best way to predict the future is to create it".

PETER DRUCKER

The time is always right to do the right thing and it is continuous action that guarantees continuous triumph in the pursuit of life. Creation of a great future is your personal responsibility which no one can do for you. Whose direction you follow determines the future you find yourself. However, to find yourself in a future you desire, you will have to take personal responsibility to create it and that can only be done by your dream.

There is nothing as powerful as a dream in the pursuit of a great future. Great men are men with great dreams who refused to give up on their dreams until they have accomplished it.

The dream you don't pursue or the one you quit or give up on, you cannot fulfill.

Meanwhile, I have taken the time to share with you some fundamental truths on how you can fulfill your own dream. I know that you have a dream and your utmost desire is to fulfill that dream, I believe that, if you will pay attention to the various principles I have shared in this book, you will not fail to have a great future created by your dream.

Also, as you know that the secrets of men are in their stories; all the great dreamers I have made reference to in this book were men who did not only have a dream, but they refused to quit in the pursuit of their dreams until they arrived at their fulfillment. It is important that you develop the attitude of never giving up, because it is a key to winning in the race of life.

Those who have won in the race of life are those who refused to quit in spite of all odds. Also, those who have failed are those who quit and gave up the pursuit of their dreams as a result of fear, procrastination and/or impatience. If you will hold on just one more time, you will discover that you are very close to your dreamland of fulfillment. It may be that the next appointment you have is what will bring you closer to the fulfillment of your long awaited desire, though several previous ones failed. Those ones that failed in the past are just part of the process that you will have to go through to get you to the one that will be successful.

Never stay in the past if you desire to fulfill your dream. That past is gone and it is in the past. It has come to pass. Move on to the future because that is where your fulfillment is. There is nothing to hold on to in what is past except for positive results of your past accomplishment.

Therefore, it is imperative that you develop the attitude of celebration of every level of result in your pursuit. It does not matter the kind or level of result – positive or negative, big or small- you need to celebrate it. It is a continuous celebration that guarantees a continuous flow of grace required to fulfill your dream. And celebration will turn negative results to positive ones.

Greatness is a product of grace at work in a man. And grace is made available through continuous celebration. God demands that we recognize Him as the source and 'fulfiller' of our dreams in life. That is why we need to acknowledge Him at every stage of the pursuit of the dream He has given us.

There is no fulfillment of dream without the hand of God. And the hand of God is provoked by the faith of man. In other words, faith is a master key to a world of fulfillment in life. Faith is a product of your belief in God and His word. However, the beginning of a life of faith that will bring fulfillment is the new life through Jesus Christ.

It is of great importance to note that there is no lasting success anywhere in this world outside of life in Christ. And as a matter of fact, true and lasting fulfillment comes from the discovery of God's purpose and pursuit of same with divinely inspired dreams.

As you seek to achieve success and lasting fulfillment, you need to understand that your connection with God, the source of all great dreams, through Jesus Christ is of utmost importance. This will determine to a great extent how you will fulfill your dream and how speedy your progress will be. Therefore, get connected to the source of life today.

GET CONNECTED

In case you are reading this book and you are yet to receive Jesus as your personal Lord and Savior, please, say these words as your act of submission to God's redemption plan:

Thank you Heavenly Father for sending Your Son Jesus to save me. Lord Jesus, I believe that you died and resurrected to save me, I ask that you come into my life today. Forgive me of my sin, cleanse me with your blood and accept me in the beloved. I confess you as my Lord and Savior today. Now I know that I am born again and saved from sin and the world. Thank you Lord for saving me. Amen

I congratulate you for making this great decision today and I pray that you will not fall apart in your walk with God in this new-found faith in Christ.

Friend, do not read this book just as one of those motivational books, take time to locate the light you need from it to fulfill your dream.

It is the Dreamers' World. Your have a dream, therefore, it is your world. You are born to rule your world and your dream is the key to ruling your world. Your dream must create a space for your name in the museum of global successful men.

You will not add your great dream to the wealth in the cemetery of the world, because the cemetery is wealthy enough.

Your dream will see the light of day. It will not end as ordinary daydream. It is your turn to be manifested as a son of God to your world as Joseph was manifested by his dream after many years.

You are welcome to a world of Impact and Exploits.

If this book has been of great blessing to you, please write us through our emails or send SMS or give us a call through our phones numbers to share your testimonies. You can also connect with us through our Facebook pages and website.

Do not fail to recommend this book to other people as a way of being a blessing to them in contributing to the fulfillment of their God-ordained purposes in life.

In addition, we welcome your comments and views about the book so as to know how we can serve you and other people in a better way.

Thank you.

Other Books By The Same Author

1. Become The Best! Release Your Potential

2. Dream Big and Succeed

3. Living Your Vision

4. Purpose Power Secrets

5. Your Dream Creates Your Future

About The Author

Sunday Adeniyi Ezekiel is an ordained Pastor, Insightful Teacher, Creative and Innovative Leadership Coach, with a visionary mandate to raise a people of impact and Exploits.

Ordained into an independent ministry by Bishop David Oyedepo of Living Faith Church a.k.a. Winners Chapel International after serving as a Pastor for some years in the headquarters in Canaan Land.

He is the President and Senior Pastor of DREAMERS WORLD CHRISTIAN CENTRE (a.k.a Faith Impact Chapel Int'l) Lagos, Nigeria.

As an astute business magnate with a passion to help people create lasting wealth, he is the co-founder, Executive Director and member of the Board of Directors of RICHLIFE COMMERCIAL AND LOGISTICTS LIMITED, a fast growing real estate company with two major brands namely RICHLIFE ESTATE AND GARDENS and RICHLIFE ROYAL CITY with over 500 network of Associates spread across Lagos, other parts of Nigeria and abroad.

He holds a Diploma in Public Accounting and Auditing from Kwara State Polytechnic, Ilorin and BSc in Business Administration from Lagos State University.

He is also a graduate of Leadership Diploma from Word of Faith Bible Institute (WOFBI) and Leadership Certificate from Daystar Leadership Academy (DLA), Lagos.

He is happily married to his lovely wife Helen who is a co-labourer in the work of the ministry. They are blessed with children; Oyindamola, Olamiposi and Olasurubomi.

www.ingramcontent.com/pod-product-compliance
Lightning Source LLC
Chambersburg PA
CBHW071445220526
45472CB00003B/672